This book is to be returned on or before
the last date stamped below.

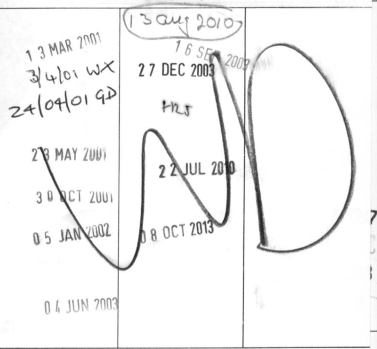

1 3 MAR 2001

3/4/01 WX

24/04/01 9D

1 3 aug 2010

1 6 SEP 2003

27 DEC 2003

HLJ

2 8 MAY 2001

3 0 OCT 2001

0 5 JAN 2002

2 2 JUL 2010

0 8 OCT 2013

0 4 JUN 2003

LEARNING FOR LIFE

D1420958

RENEWALS   Please quote: date of return, your ticket number
and computer label number for each item.

Selected Poems

Sonnets p 216
3
6   5
7
8
9
10
+ onwards

Selected Poems of

Elizabeth Barrett Browning

SELECTED AND
WITH AN INTRODUCTION AND
PREFACES BY
MARGARET FORSTER

Chatto & Windus
LONDON

Published in 1988 by
Chatto & Windus Limited
30 Bedford Square
London WC1B 3RP

A CIP catalogue record for this book is available
from the British Library
ISBN 0-7011 3311 2

Designed by Humphrey Stone
Photoset by Rowland Phototypesetting Ltd,
Bury St Edmunds, Suffolk
Printed in Great Britain by
Redwood Burn Ltd,
Trowbridge, Wiltshire

Acknowledgements

I would like to thank Isobel Armstrong, Alethea Hayter, Angela Leighton and Dorothy Mermin for their interest, advice and encouragement.

Contents

(*See Note on the Text)

Introduction

Elizabeth Barrett, who was born near Durham on 6th March 1806, began writing poetry as a child. Her first extant poem is a birthday ode written to her mother on 1st May 1814. Six years later, on her fourteenth birthday, her father paid to have published fifty copies of *The Battle of Marathon*, her 1,164 line epic. Her name was not on the volume but it was common practice then to publish anonymously. By the time she wrote this she was sure that poetry was her vocation: she was no lady scribbler amusing herself during idle afternoons. Poetry, in her opinion, was responsible work and poets, she believed, were required to "tell the real truth" about the world in which they lived.

Until she was forty, Elizabeth Barrett knew very little about the world. She lived from 1809–1832 with her family at Hope End, near Ledbury in Herefordshire, where her father had had built, in a remote rural situation, a magnificent house of Turkish design. Mr. Barrett, whose wealth came from Jamaican sugar plantations, thought his family should be self-sufficient but since he had eleven children, and the house was usually full of visiting relatives, Hope End was never lonely. Elizabeth had a gregarious and boisterous childhood, enjoying every kind of outdoor game and activity—she had as much taste for rolling in hay lofts as for writing verses.

At the age of fifteen, Elizabeth had measles and shortly afterwards an undiagnosed illness. Her doctors, unable to decide what was the matter with her, sent her to the Gloucester Spa for treatment. She stayed there almost a year, convinced she had a spine complaint. Her doctors disagreed. Correspondence between them reveals that they thought it best to treat their patient "*as if for*" (their words) a spine disease although they could find no evidence for it. When Elizabeth returned home, aged sixteen, weak from spending so many months in bed, she was greatly changed. She was extremely depressed and missed her favourite brother Edward, known as Bro, who had been sent to Charterhouse. Without Bro, who alone of her brothers and sisters shared her intellectual interests, Elizabeth was lonely. Poetry began to take on a deeper significance and became for her "where we live and have our being".

From 1821, when she was only fifteen, Elizabeth's poems began to appear in the leading literary magazines of the day (such as *New Monthly Magazine*). This gave her considerable pleasure and brought her to the attention of her peers. For the next decade the friends she made through her poems appearing in magazines sustained her in a life that was increasingly introverted. She did not meet any of her new correspondents, who wrote congratulating her on her poetry, with the exception of Hugh Boyd who lived nearby. Boyd, a blind Greek scholar who was married with a daughter almost the same age as Elizabeth, wrote to her after the publication of her second privately published volume, *An Essay on Mind, with Other Poems* (1826). Elizabeth persuaded her father to allow her to visit Boyd at his home near Malvern and spent many happy hours reading Greek to him. Apart from Boyd, she met no men outside her family and the close circle of her Hope End neighbourhood. She did not wish to—her poor health, ever since her adolescent illness, gave her the excuse to shut herself away and do nothing but read and write. The sudden death of her mother, in 1828, naturally deepened her sense of futility. If it had not been for her strong religious faith and for her poetry she felt she would have welcomed death herself: "Death has such a pleading tongue in what is called its silence."

In 1832, the Barretts left Hope End. The plantations in Jamaica, upon which the family wealth depended, were not yielding the same income since the passing of the act to abolish slavery, and Mr. Barrett was obliged to sell his Hope End house and estate. He went to London, from where he directed his

Jamaican business, and his family went first to Sidmouth. They were there for three years, with Mr. Barrett making frequent lengthy visits to see them. At the end of 1835 the family were reunited with their father in London (first in a rented house and then in 50 Wimpole Street, purchased in April 1838). London brought Elizabeth within the reach of numerous literary contacts. A distant cousin, John Kenyon, a minor poet and an influential literary patron and host, visited her and, discovering her shyness tried to help her overcome it. He arranged for her to meet the writer Mary Russell Mitford, whose *Our Village (Sketches of Country Life)* had made her famous, and even succeeded in persuading her to attend a dinner party where she met Wordsworth and Walter Savage Landor—it was a night, she wrote, when she "walked among stars".

But in spite of these new social opportunities London had one grave defect: its climate was bad for Elizabeth's health. She began to cough and in 1838 she almost died when a lung haemorrhaged. The doctor advised her to leave London to recuperate. She did not wish to do so partly because she did not wish to split up the family and partly because she was relishing the success of her new volume of poetry, *The Seraphim, and Other Poems*, the first volume to appear under her own name, published by Saunders and Otley on 6th June 1838. But she failed to recover and was obliged to leave London in August for Torquay. Here she spent the most miserable three years of her life, from 1838 to 1841. She seemed unable to regain her strength and then, in July 1840, Bro, who had been allowed by Mr. Barrett to stay with her, was drowned. He went out fishing with some friends and their boat was wrecked in a sudden violent storm. The shock devastated Elizabeth. For three months she lay in a darkened room incapable of speech or thought, and with no desire to go on living. The gradual realization that grief was not going to kill her forced her to the conclusion that God must have some purpose in allowing her to live. She became convinced that this purpose was to write poetry. "All the life and strength which are in me," she wrote, "seem to have passed into my poetry. It is my *pou sto*—not to move the world; but to live on."

In September 1841 she was taken back to 50 Wimpole Street in a specially designed invalid carriage and was reunited with her family. She devoted herself to her poetry, anxious to make up for lost time, and in 1844 published a collection in two volumes, entitled simply *Poems*, which made her name. The longest and by far the most ambitious poem in the collection was "A Drama of Exile", on the subject of Adam and Eve's expulsion from the garden of Eden, but this received far less critical attention than the other sixty poems in the volumes. The poem which was most greatly liked by both critics and friends was a ballad, "Lady Geraldine's Courtship". In it, Elizabeth Barrett paid tribute to a young poet, Robert Browning, whose work Lady Geraldine reads and admires. She herself had been reading Browning since 1835 when he published *Paracelsus*. John Kenyon, knowing of her interest in Browning's work, had offered to introduce her to him but she had declined the tempting invitation. But now, after he had read her 1844 *Poems*, Browning wrote to her. The two poets corresponded for five months before Elizabeth allowed Robert to visit her. They fell in love at once but it was sixteen months before they were secretly married, on 12th September 1846, and then left for Italy, exactly one week later. Elizabeth left behind her letters explaining her actions—to her sisters, to her brothers, and to her father of whose certain anger she was terrified.

Elizabeth's life changed completely and dramatically. She exchanged her Wimpole Street room for the Casa Guidi, the greyness of London for the brilliant sun of Florence. She was now a happily married woman but, although for a while she felt disinclined to write, she had not forgotten her vocation. In the autumn of 1848 she composed what became Part One of *Casa Guidi Windows*. This long poem was a dramatic departure from her previous work; it was not the first time she had attempted a political subject but it was the first time she openly acknowledged herself to be politically engaged. Previously, she had described social evils (as in "The Cry of the Children", 1843) but she had been detached from the political situation in which these flourished. Now she saw herself as involved, commenting powerfully and controversially on political events and seeking to change what was happening through the medium of her poetry. On 12th September 1847, her first wedding anniversary, the Florentines had been granted certain civil rights by their Grand Duke. She watched the magnificent procession, held to celebrate this, from the balcony of her home in the Casa Guidi. It thrilled and excited her to see the cause of Italian unity and freedom from Austrian oppression apparently advance and gain ground throughout the country. She saw her poetry, from this moment, as a weapon with which she could help to fight for this cause. It was, to her, a form of direct action. Her work had always been passionate, springing from deeply personal religious feeling, but now the emotional element was matched by a harder, more objective tone. This controlled intensity was evident, too, in her epic *Aurora Leigh* (1856): *Aurora Leigh* brought to fruition all her talents—it was both personal and political, subjective as well as objective, in parts lyrical and in others declamatory.

But by the time she came to write *Aurora Leigh*, Elizabeth Barrett Browning was once more very ill. During the first five years of her marriage, which had included the birth of her son Pen in 1849, Elizabeth had enjoyed better health than she had ever done in her adult life. Then in July 1850 she had her fourth miscarriage which almost proved fatal (her doctor told Robert his wife had lost "above a hundred ounces of blood" in twenty-four hours). She made a remarkable recovery but was never as strong again. A visit to England, where her father's intransigence made her wretched, and a winter of unexpected severity in Paris, pulled her down further. Robert took her to Rome in November 1853 for six months but, although the mild climate helped her congested lungs, she was still unwell. The slightest cold triggered off lung infections (though there is no conclusive evidence that she had TB). Further visits to England, to see work through the printers and to visit her sisters whom she missed very much, had disastrous psychological effects. Her father still refused to forgive her and she slowly began to acknowledge that he never would. In 1857, soon after the immensely successful publication of *Aurora Leigh*, Mr. Barrett died. The distress this caused his unforgiven daughter sapped her strength still further. She managed to travel to Brittany the following summer to join Robert's family and some of her own but returned exhausted to Italy in the autumn. Another winter was spent in Rome but Elizabeth hardly left her bed. In the early summer she returned to the Casa Guidi in Florence where she died on 29th June 1861, aged fifty five, in Robert's arms.

*　　*　　*

During her life, Elizabeth Barrett Browning achieved widespread acclaim for her poetry though not quite as widespread as is commonly supposed. One of the most often-repeated "facts" about her is that she was supposedly "widely-canvassed" for the post of Poet Laureate when Wordsworth died in 1850. This is untrue. Her name was merely suggested, patronisingly, as part of a campaign against the very existence of the post of Poet Laureate. *The Athenaeum*, in its gossip column for the April 1850 issue, poured scorn on the appointment of Poet Laureate whose duties it alleged "belong to the times of court jesters". The May issue continued to abuse the office and by June was referring to it as "an unmeaning piece of buffoonery". It did not matter, *The Athenaeum* maintained, who was appointed because the post was "meaningless" and "any poet—or indeed no poet—may do as well as any other". It was in this dismissive context that Elizabeth Barrett Browning's name was mentioned.

Her name, nevertheless, did stand high during the 1850s. The same *Athenaeum* referred to her late in 1850 as "probably, of her sex, the first imaginative writer England has produced in any age—she is, beyond comparison, the first poetess of her own". The key phrase was "of her sex". Half the praise lavished on Elizabeth Barrett Browning was bestowed because she was a woman. Before 1838, when she published the first collection under her own name, few women had been generally acclaimed as poets. The first to make any significant mark were the seventeenth-century writers Aphra Benn, Anne Finch and Katherine Philips. To that small number the eighteenth-century added Charlotte Smith and Joanna Baillie who was still writing when Elizabeth Barrett Browning was born and whom she greatly admired. "It is a strong impression with me," commented Elizabeth in 1845, "that previous to Joanna Baillie there was no such thing in England as a poetess; and that so far from triumphing over the rest of the world in that particular product we lay until then under the feet of the world." She herself, she wrote, looked everywhere for poetic "grand-mothers" and could find none. She thought of herself as isolated both when she looked back and when she looked round at her female contemporaries of whom she admired only Mrs. Hemans and Letitia Landon.

Elizabeth Barrett Browning realized that as a woman she had a special function as a poet, that she had a responsibility to become the "grandmother" she herself had sought. Her early poetry had done little to "represent the age" for women but in her 1844 collection she began, as she put it, "to speak out". She believed that she ought to speak about women's sufferings and social position, that if women writers did not acknowledge this duty then, so she wrote, they had "better use a pen no more" but instead "subside into slavery and concubinage". From 1844 she addressed herself to the evils of prostitution and its implicit exploitation, betrayal and humiliation of women; she explored sexual passion, maternal love and the comforts of domesticity; and she tried to analyse the relationship between a woman's art and her biological nature in order to see whether one complemented the other or whether they were mutually destructive.

If Elizabeth Barrett Browning's views on her position as a

woman poet were challenging so was her approach to poetic form. She irritated many critics with her unorthodox rhymes but defended these firmly. Her friend R. H. Horne said he really could not accept "panther" rhymed with "saunter" (in "The Dead Pan") but Elizabeth saw no objection. "If I deal too much in licences," she wrote, "it is not because I am idle but because I am speculative for freedom's sake." The same wish to be "speculative" led her to invent new words and to break regular rhythms. She was also "speculative" in the verse forms she chose. She attempted every kind of form—lyrics, blank verse, ballads and sonnets—refusing to believe that women should be restricted to those forms thought most suitable (lyrics and ballads for preference). Most daring of all was her decision to write "a poem of a new class" as she described *Aurora Leigh* ten years before she wrote it. This was to be a "novel-poem" and its influence, in creating what amounted to a new genre, was powerful. Men could no longer assume women to be limited to certain kinds of "easy" verse; women were inspired to follow the lead given to them; and poetry had to admit a new category.

*　　*　　*

Since her death in 1861, Elizabeth Barrett Browning's reputation has been insecure. She has never been entirely "lost" but she was rapidly demoted from the position she held in her life. After 1902 there was no new edition of *Aurora Leigh* until 1978, and although *Sonnets from the Portuguese*—the love poems written for Robert during their courtship in 1845–6, but not published until 1850—has been fairly regularly reprinted no collected editions of her poems have appeared since 1919. Virginia Woolf (*The Common Reader*, 1932) wrote that Elizabeth Barrett Browning had been relegated to the servants' hall of literature and only recently has the situation begun to change. Alethea Hayter predicted in 1968 that women would rescue Elizabeth Barrett Browning from the dismal servants' hall because they would eventually tune in to her "unusual wavelength". The feminist movement of the 1970s did indeed "tune in". It was not only *Aurora Leigh* that was rediscovered; the ballads, too, were found to have subversive contemporary significance. It can be argued that it is inaccurate to call Elizabeth Barrett Browning a feminist poet: the word was not in use in her day and she herself expressed some decidedly non-feminist opinions. But it is nevertheless an appropriate term because in all her poetry from 1844 feminist themes are strong: the oppression women suffer at the hands of men is explored and condemned again and again. This selection has been chosen to illustrate those themes among the many others which make up the work of Elizabeth Barrett Browning. She wanted, above all, to "tell the truth" and to tell it in particular for women. "If a woman ignores these wrongs, then may women as a sex continue to suffer them; there is no help for any of us—let us be dumb and die. I have spoken therefore and in speaking have used plain words . . ."

Note on the Text

The following selected poems, with the exception of "A True Dream", are taken from the *Oxford Complete Edition of the Poetical Works of Elizabeth Barrett Browning* (Henry Frowde, OUP, 1908). Stanzas are arranged and numbered as they were in the poet's original editions. "A True Dream", written while Elizabeth Barrett was at Sidmouth in 1833, did not appear during her life. It belongs chronologically before *The Seraphim and Other Poems*. It is difficult to understand why it was not included in that volume since there was nothing in the subject matter to bar it; the reason can only have been that, in the author's opinion, it fell short of her own high standards. It appears in *New Poems by Robert and Mrs. Browning*, edited by F. G. Kenyon (1914).

"De Profundis" was written in 1841 but not published in this country until after Elizabeth Barrett Browning's death. It appeared in *Last Poems*, but I have positioned it chronologically in this collection.

"Question and Answer" and "A Denial" did not appear until 1856 when they were included in the fourth edition of the 1850 *Poems*.

Sonnets from the Portuguese were so called in an attempt to make people believe they were translations: both Brownings thought these poems too personal to be published under the name of Elizabeth Barrett Browning. In the 1850 *Poems* there are forty-three sonnets. The sonnet previously called "Future and Past", which appeared divorced from *Sonnets from the Portuguese* in the 1850 collection, was added to them as No. XLII in 1856, bringing the number up to forty-four.

Casa Guidi Windows, Part One was originally entitled

"Meditation in Tuscany". It was completed in 1848 but not published until 1851 when Part Two was written.

Last Poems was published posthumously in 1862, the year after Elizabeth Barrett Browning's death.

In this selection there are no extracts from either *Aurora Leigh* or any of Elizabeth Barrett Browning's longer poems. *Aurora Leigh* is easily accessible today and the longer poems —such as "The Battle of Marathon", "The Seraphim" and "Drama of Exile"—suffer severely in extract form. Elizabeth Barrett Browning herself disliked extracts: a poem, to her, was an entity and she preferred the whole or nothing.

Selected Poems of
Elizabeth Barrett Browning

Poems Selected from

AN ESSAY ON MIND,
WITH OTHER POEMS
(1826)

Preface

Elizabeth Barrett was in the habit, from the age of eight, of writing birthday odes to every member of the large Barrett family (her father referred to her as the Poet Laureate of Hope End). "To My Father on His Birthday" is in this tradition. It pleased her mother very much: she commented that these lines were "a just tribute".

An Essay on Mind was eighty-eight pages long but in spite of this impressive length, and its great seriousness, it was the fourteen short poems, which appeared with it, that attracted more interest. Elizabeth assumed this was because the shorter pieces were easier to read.

"Song" went into many commonplace books. Its advice —"Trust not to Joy"—was to be the theme she developed steadily during the next decade. When she wrote this poem she had endured no personal tragedies, which makes her cynicism surprising. It sprang instead from her struggle to accept the confines of her own life.

"The Dream" was her father's favourite: he liked its "highly poetic beauty". The rhyme and metre are conventional but there is a passion and impetuosity in the writing which show what Elizabeth Barrett later called her "real self pecking through the shell". Some of the bizarre imagery in this poem is similar to imagery common in work written under the influence of opium. There is no evidence to prove she ever wrote while under the influence of opium but it is true that she took laudanum nightly from the age of fifteen.

TO MY FATHER ON HIS BIRTHDAY

Causa fuit Pater his
HORACE

Amidst the days of pleasant mirth,
That throw their halo round our earth;
Amidst the tender thoughts that rise
To call bright tears to happy eyes;
Amidst the silken words that move
To syllable the names we love;
There glides no day of gentle bliss
More soothing to the heart than *this!*
No thoughts of fondness e'er appear
More fond, than those I write of here!
No name can e'er on tablet shine,
My Father! more beloved than *thine!*
      'Tis sweet, adown the shady past,
A lingering look of love to cast—
Back th' enchanted world to call,
That beamed around us first of all;
And walk with Memory fondly o'er
The paths where Hope had been before—
Sweet to receive the sylphic sound
That breathes in tenderness around,
Repeating to the listening ear
The names that made our childhood dear—
For parted Joy, like Echo, kind,
Will leave her dulcet voice behind,
To tell, amidst the magic air,
How oft she smiled and lingered there.
Oh! let the deep Aonian shell
Breathe tuneful numbers, clear and well,
While the glad Hours, in fair array,
Lead on this buxom Holiday;
And Time, as on his way he springs
Hates the last bard who gave him wings;

For 'neath thy gentleness of praise,
My Father! rose my early lays!
And when the lyre was scarce awake,
I loved its strings for *thy* loved sake;
Wooed the kind Muses—but the while
Thought only how to win thy smile—
My proudest fame—my dearest pride—
More dear than all the world beside!
And now, perchance, I seek the tone
For magic that is more its own;
But still my Father's looks remain
The best Maecenas of my strain;
My gentlest joy, upon his brow
To read the smile, that meets me now—
To hear him, in his kindness, say
The words,—perchance he'll speak today!

SONG

Weep, as if you thought of laughter!
Smile, as tears were coming after!
Marry your pleasures to your woes;
And think life's green well worth its rose!

No sorrow will your heart betide,
Without a comfort by its side;
The sun may sleep in his sea-bed,
But you have starlight overhead.

Trust not to Joy! the rose of June,
When opened wide, will wither soon;
Italian days without twilight
Will turn them suddenly to night.

Joy, most changeful of all things,
Flits away on rainbow wings;
And when they look the gayest, know,
It is that they are spread to go!

THE DREAM

A FRAGMENT

I had a dream!—my spirit was unbound
From the dark iron of its dungeon, clay,
And rode the steeds of Time;—my thoughts had sound,
And spoke without a word,—I went away
Among the buried ages, and did lay
The pulses of my heart beneath the touch
Of the rude minstrel Time, that he should play
Thereon a melody which might seem such
As musing spirits love—mournful, but not too much!

I had a dream—and there mine eyes did see
The shadows of past deeds like present things—
The sepulchres of Greece and Hespery,
Aegyptus, and old lands, gave up their kings,
Their prophets, saints, and minstrels, whose lute-strings
Keep a long echo—yea, the dead, white bones
Did stand up by the house whereto Death clings,
And dressed themselves in life, speaking of thrones,
And fame, and power, and beauty, in familiar tones!

I went back further still, for I beheld
What time the earth was one fair Paradise—
And over such bright meads the waters welled,
I wot the rainbow was content to rise
Upon the earth, when absent from the skies!
And there were tall trees that I never knew,
Whereon sate nameless birds in merry guise,
Folding their radiant wings, as the flowers do,
When summer nights send sleep down with the dew.

*   *   *

Anon there came a change—a terrible motion,
That made all living things grow pale and shake!
The dark Heavens bowed themselves unto the ocean,
Like a strong man in strife—Ocean did take
His flight across the mountains; and the lake
Was lashed into a sea where the winds ride—
Earth was no more, for in her merry-make
She had forgot her God—Sin claimed his bride,
And with his vampire breath sucked out her life's fair tide!

Life went back to her nostrils, and she raised
Her spirit from the waters once again—
The lovely sights, on which I erst had gazed,
Were *not*—though she was beautiful as when
The Grecian called her 'Beauty'—sinful men
Walked i' the track of the waters, and felt bold—
Yea, they looked up to Heaven in calm disdain,
As if no eye had seen its vault unfold,
Darkness, and fear, and death!—as if a tale were told!

And ages fled away within my dream;
And still Sin made the heart his dwelling-place,
Eclipsing Heaven from men; but it would seem
That two or three dared commune face to face,
And speak of the soul's life, of hope, and grace.
Anon there rose such sounds as angels breathe—
For a God came to die, bringing down peace—
'Pan *was not*'; and the darkness that did wreathe
The earth, passed from the soul—Life came by Death!

*   *   *

Poems Selected from

PROMETHEUS BOUND

Translated from the Greek of Æschylus.
And Miscellaneous Poems

(1833)

Preface

Elizabeth Barrett's translation of Aeschylus was scathingly reviewed. ("We advise those who adventure in the hazardous lists of poetic translation to touch any one other than Aeschylus: and they may take warning by the author before us.") The nineteen shorter pieces in the volume were preferred. Some, like "The Image of God", were deeply religious but the collection also included some fine nature poems. "A Sea-Side Meditation" contains many examples of Elizabeth's growing fondness for double adjectives, reversing of words, and arcane vocabulary.

The most original poem in the collection was "The Tempest". While the Barretts were still living at Hope End there was a violent storm in which a tree was struck by lightning and two women killed nearby. Twenty years later, Elizabeth described to Robert Browning how terrified she had been. Critics have found in this poem plain indications of severe psychological trauma which, they allege, the poet used the image of a storm to explore. The hated one, who also hates, has been variously identified as Elizabeth's father or her brother Bro, though all the biographical evidence would suggest this is untrue. The lurid visual images in "The Tempest" make this the most powerful of all Elizabeth Barrett's early work.

EPITAPH

Beauty, who softly walkest all thy days
In silken garment to the tunes of praise;—
Lover, whose dreamings by the green-banked river,
Where once she wandered, fain would last for ever;—
King, whom the nations scan, adoring scan,
And shout 'a god,' when sin hath marked thee man;—
Bard, on whose brow the Hyblan dew remains,
Albeit the fever burneth in the veins;—
Hero, whose sword in tyrant's blood is hot;—
Sceptic, who doubting, wouldst be doubted not;—
Man, whosoe'er thou art, whate'er thy trust;—
Respect thyself in me;—thou treadest *dust*.

THE IMAGE OF GOD

I am God, and there is none like me.
ISAIAH xlvi.9
Christ, who is the image of God.
2 CORINTHIANS iv.4

Thou! art thou like to God?
(I asked this question of the glorious sun)
Thou high unwearied one,
Whose course in heat, and light, and life is run?

Eagles may view thy face—clouds can assuage
Thy fiery wrath—the sage
Can mete thy stature—thou shalt fade with age.
Thou art not like to God.

[13]

Thou! art thou like to God?
(I asked this question of the bounteous earth)
O thou, who givest birth
To forms of beauty and to sounds of mirth?

In all thy glory works the worm decay—
Thy golden harvests stay
For seed and toil—thy power shall pass away.
Thou art not like to God.

Thou! art thou like to God?
(I asked this question of my deathless soul)
O thou, whose musings roll
Above the thunder, o'er creation's whole?

Thou art not. Sin, and shame, and agony
Within thy deepness lie:
They utter forth their voice in thee, and cry,
'*Thou* art not like to God.'

Then art Thou like to God;
Thou, who didst bear the sin, and shame, and woe—
O Thou, whose sweat did flow—
Whose tears did gush—whose brow was dead and low?

No grief is like Thy grief; no heart can prove
Love like unto Thy love;
And none, save only Thou,—below, above,—
O God, is like to God!

A SEA-SIDE MEDITATION

Ut per aquas quae nunc rerum simulacra videmus
LUCRETIUS

Go, travel 'mid the hills! The summer's hand
Hath shaken pleasant freshness o'er them all.
Go, travel 'mid the hills! There, tuneful streams
Are touching myriad stops, invisible;
And winds, and leaves, and birds, and your own thoughts
(Not the least glad) in wordless chorus, crowd
Around the thymele of Nature.
                                    Go,
And travel onward. Soon shall leaf and bird,
Wind, stream, no longer sound. Thou shalt behold
Only the pathless sky, and houseless sward;
O'er which anon are spied innumerous sails
Of fisher vessels like the wings o' the hill,
And white as gulls above them, and as fast,—
But sink they—sink they out of sight. And now
The wind is springing upward in your face;
And, with its fresh-toned gushings, you may hear
Continuous sound which is not of the wind,
Nor of the thunder, nor o' the cataract's
Deep passion, nor o' the earthquake's wilder pulse;
But which rolls on in stern tranquillity,
As memories of evil o'er the soul;—
Boweth the bare broad Heaven.—What view you? sea—
        and sea!

The sea—the glorious sea! from side to side
Swinging the grandeur of his foamy strength,
And undersweeping the horizon,—on—
On—with his life and voice inscrutable.
Pause: sit you down in silence! I have read
Of that Athenian, who, when ocean raged,
Unchained the prisoned music of his lips

[15]

By shouting to the billows, sound for sound.
I marvel how his mind would let his tongue
Affront thereby the ocean's solemnness.
Are we not mute, or speak restrainedly,
When overhead the trampling tempests go,
Dashing their lightning from their hoofs? and when
We stand beside the bier? and when we see
The strong bow down to weep—and stray among
Places which dust or mind hath sanctified?
Yea! for such sights and acts do tear apart
The close and subtle clasping of a chain,
Formed not of gold, but of corroded brass,
Whose links are furnished from the common mine
Of every day's event, and want, and wish;
From work-times, diet-times, and sleeping-times:
And thence constructed, mean and heavy links
Within the pandemonic walls of sense
Enchain our deathless part, constrain our strength,
And waste the goodly stature of our soul.

Howbeit, we love this bondage; we do cleave
Unto the sordid and unholy thing,
Fearing the sudden wrench required to break
Those clasped links. Behold! all sights and sounds
In air, and sea, and earth, and under earth,
All flesh, all life, all ends, are mysteries;
And all that is mysterious dreadful seems,
And all we cannot understand we fear.
Ourselves do scare ourselves: we hide our sight
In artificial nature from the true,
And throw sensation's veil associative
On God's creation, man's intelligence;
Bowing our high imaginings to eat
Dust, like the serpent, once erect as they;
Binding conspicuous on our reason's brow
Phylacteries of shame; learning to feel

By rote, and act by rule (man's rule, not God's!),
Unto our words grow echoes, and our thoughts
A mechanism of spirit.
                              Can this last?
No! not for ay. We cannot subject ay
The heaven-born spirit to the earth-born flesh.
Tame lions *will* scent blood, and appetite
Carnivorous glare from out their restless eyes.
Passions, emotions, sudden changes, throw
Our nature back upon us, till we burn.
What warmed Cyrene's fount? As poets sing,
The *change* from light to dark, from dark to light.

All that doth force this nature back on us,
All that doth force the mind to view the mind,
Engend'reth what is named by men, *sublime*.
Thus when, our wonted valley left, we gain
The mountain's horrent brow, and mark from thence
The sweep of lands extending with the sky;
Or view the spanless plain; or turn our sight
Upon yon deep's immensity;—we breathe
As if our breath were marble: to and fro
Do reel our pulses, and our words are mute.
We cannot mete by parts, but grapple all;
We cannot measure with our eye, but soul;
And fear is on us. The extent unused,
Our spirit, sends, to spirit's element,
To seize upon abstraction: first on space,
The which *eternity in place* I deem;
And then upon eternity; till thought
Hath formed a mirror from their secret sense,
Wherein we view ourselves, and back recoil
At our own awful likeness; ne'ertheless,
Cling to that likeness with a wonder wild,
And while we tremble, glory—proud in fear.
So ends the prose of life: and so shall be

[17]

Unlocked her poetry's magnific store.
And so, thou pathless and perpetual sea,
So, o'er thy deeps, I brooded and must brood,
Whether I view thee in thy dreadful peace,
Like a spent warrior hanging in the sun
His glittering arms, and meditating death;
Or whether thy wild visage gath'reth shades,
What time thou marshall'st forth thy waves who hold
A covenant of storms, then roar and wind
Under the racking rocks; as martyrs lie
Wheel-bound; and, dying, utter lofty words!
Whether the strength of day is young and high,
Or whether, weary of the watch, he sits
Pale on thy wave, and weeps himself to death;—
In storm and calm, at morn and eventide,
Still have I stood beside thee, and out-thrown
My spirit onward on thine element,—
Beyond thine element,—to tremble low
Before those feet which trod thee as they trod
Earth,—to the holy, happy, peopled place,
Where there is no more sea. Yea, and my soul,
Having put on thy vast similitude,
Hath wildly moaned at her proper depth,
Echoed her proper musings, veiled in shade
Her secrets of decay, and exercised
An elemental strength, in casting up
Rare gems and things of death on fancy's shore,
Till Nature said 'Enough.'
                              Who longest dreams,
Dreams not for ever; seeing day and night
And corporal feebleness divide his dreams,
And on his elevate creations weigh
With hunger, cold, heat, darkness, weariness:
Else should we be like gods; else would the course
Of thought's free wheels, increased in speed and might
By an eterne volution, oversweep

The heights of wisdom, and invade her depths:
So, knowing all things, should we have all power;
For is not Knowledge power? But mighty spells
Our operation sear; the Babel must,
Or ere it touch the sky, fall down to earth:
The web, half formed, must tumble from our hands,
And, ere they can resume it, lie decayed.
Mind struggles vainly from the flesh. E'en so,
Hell's angel (saith a scroll apocryphal)
Shall, when the latter days of earth have shrunk
Before the blast of God, affect his heaven;
Lift his scarred brow, confirm his rebel heart,
Shoot his strong wings, and darken pole and pole,—
Till day be blotted into night; and shake
The fevered clouds, as if a thousand storms
Throbbed into life! Vain hope—vain strength—vain flight!
God's arm shall meet God's foe, and hurl him back!

IDOLS

How weak the gods of this world are—
    And weaker yet their worship made me!
I have been an idolater
    Of three—and three times they betrayed me!

Mine oldest worshipping was given
    To natural Beauty, ay residing
In bowery earth and starry heaven,
    In ebbing sea, and river gliding.

But natural Beauty shuts her bosom
    To what the natural feelings tell!
Albeit I sighed, the trees would blossom—
    Albeit I smiled, the blossoms fell.

Then left I earthly sights, to wander
    Amid a grove of name divine,
Where bay-reflecting streams meander,
    And Moloch Fame hath reared a shrine.

Not green, but black, is that reflection;
    On rocky beds those waters lie;
That grove hath chillness and dejection—
    How could I sing? I had to sigh.

Last, human Love, thy Lares greeting,
    To rest and warmth I vowed my years.
To rest? how wild my pulse is beating!
    To warmth? ah me! my burning tears.

Aye, *they* may burn—though thou be frozen
    By death, and changes wint'ring on!
Fame!—Beauty!—idols madly chosen—
    Were yet of gold; but *thou* art STONE!

Crumble like stone! my voice no longer
    Shall wail their names, who silent be:
There is a voice that soundeth stronger—
    'My daughter, give thine heart to *Me*.'

Lord! take mine heart! O first and fairest,
    Whom all creation's ends shall hear;
Who deathless love in death declarest!
    None else is beauteous—famous—dear!

THE TEMPEST

A FRAGMENT

Mors erat ante oculos.
LUCAN lib. ix

*   *   *

The forest made my home—the voiceful streams
My minstrel throng: the everlasting hills,—
Which marry with the firmament, and cry
Unto the brazen thunder, 'Come away,
Come from thy secret place, and try our strength,'—
Enwrapped me with their solemn arms. Here, light
Grew pale as darkness, scarèd by the shade
O' the forest Titans. Here, in piny state,
Reigned Night, the Aethiopian queen, and crowned
The charmèd brow of Solitude, her spouse.

*   *   *

A sign was on creation. You beheld
All things encoloured in a sulph'rous hue,
As day were sick with fear. The haggard clouds
O'erhung the utter lifelessness of air;
The top boughs of the forest, all aghast,
Stared in the face of Heaven; the deep-mouthed wind,
That hath a voice to bay the armèd sea,
Fled with a low cry like a beaten hound;
And only that askance the shadows flew
Some open-beakèd birds in wilderment,
Naught stirred abroad. All dumb did Nature seem,
In expectation of the coming storm.

It came in power. You soon might hear afar
The footsteps of the martial thunder sound
Over the mountain battlements; the sky
Being deep-stained with hues fantastical,
Red like to blood, and yellow like to fire,
And black like plumes at funerals; overhead

[21]

You might behold the lightning faintly gleam
Amid the clouds which thrill and gape aside,
And straight again shut up their solemn jaws,
As if to interpose between Heaven's wrath
And Earth's despair. Interposition brief!
Darkness is gathering out her mighty pall
Above us, and the pent-up rain is loosed,
Down trampling in its fierce delirium.

Was not my spirit gladdened, as with wine,
To hear the iron rain, and view the mark
Of battle on the banner of the clouds?
Did I not hearken for the battle-cry,
And rush along the bowing woods to meet
The riding Tempest—skyey cataracts
Hissing around him with rebellion vain?
Yea! and I lifted up my glorying voice
In an 'All hail'; when, wildly resonant,
As brazen chariots rushing from the war,
As passioned waters gushing from the rock,
As thousand crashèd woods, the thunder cried:
And at his cry the forest tops were shook
As by the woodman's axe; and far and near
Staggered the mountains with a muttered dread.

All hail unto the lightning! hurriedly
His lurid arms are glaring through the air,
Making the face of Heaven to show like hell!
Let him go breathe his sulphur stench about,
And, pale with death's own mission, lord the storm!
Again the gleam—the glare: I turned to hail
Death's mission: at my feet there lay the dead!

The dead—the dead lay there! I could not view
(For Night espoused the storm, and made all dark)
Its features, but the lightning in its course

[22]

Shivered above a white and corpse-like heap,
Stretched in the path, as if to show his prey,
And have a triumph ere he passed. Then I
Crouched down upon the ground, and groped about
Until I touched that thing of flesh, rain-drenched,
And chill, and soft. Nathless, I did refrain
My soul from natural horror! I did lift
The heavy head, half-bedded in the clay,
Unto my knee; and passed my fingers o'er
The wet face, touching every lineament,
Until I found the brow; and chafed its chill,
To know if life yet lingered in its pulse.
And while I was so busied, there did leap
From out the entrails of the firmament,
The lightning, who his white unblenching breath
Blew in the dead man's face, discovering it
As by a staring day. I knew that face—
His, who did hate me—his, whom I did hate!

I shrunk not—spake not—sprang not from the ground!
But felt my lips shake without cry or breath,
And mine heart wrestle in my breast to still
The tossing of its pulses; and a cold,
Instead of living blood, o'ercreep my brow.
Albeit such darkness brooded all around,
I had dread knowledge that the open eyes
Of that dead man were glaring up to mine,
With their unwinking, unexpressive stare;
And mine I could not shut nor turn away
The man was my familiar. I had borne
Those eyes to scowl on me their living hate,

Better than I could bear their deadliness:
I had endured the curses of those lips
Far better than their silence. Oh, constrained
And awful silence!—awful peace of death!

There is an answer to all questioning,
That one word—*death*. Our bitterness can throw
No look upon the face of death, and live.
The burning thoughts that erst my soul illumed
Were quenched at once; as tapers in a pit
Wherein the vapour-witches weirdly reign
In charge of darkness. Farewell all the past!
It was out-blotted from my memory's eyes
When clay's cold silence pleaded for its sin.

Farewell the elemental war! farewell
The clashing of the shielded clouds—the cry
Of scathèd echoes! I no longer knew
Silence from sound, but wandered far away
Into the deep Eleusis of mine heart,
To learn its secret things. When armèd foes
Meet on one deck with impulse violent,
The vessel quakes thro' all her oaken ribs,
And shivers in the sea; so with mine heart:
For there had battled in her solitudes,
Contrary spirits; sympathy with power,
And stooping unto power;—the energy
And passiveness,—the thunder and the death!

Within me was a nameless thought: it closed
The Janus of my soul on echoing hinge,
And said 'Peace!' with a voice like War's. I bowed,
And trembled at its voice: it gave a key,
Empowered to open out all mysteries
Of soul and flesh; of men, who doth begin,
But endeth not; of life, and *after life*.

     *   *   *

Day came at last: her light showed grey and sad,
As hatched by tempest, and could scarce prevail
Over the shaggy forest to imprint
Its outline on the sky—expressionless,

[24]

Almost sans shadow as sans radiance:
An idiocy of light. I wakened from
My deep unslumb'ring dream, but uttered naught.
My living I uncoupled from the dead,
And looked out, 'mid the swart and sluggish air,
For place to make a grave. A mighty tree
Above me, his gigantic arms outstretched,
Poising the clouds. A thousand muttered spells
Of every ancient wind and thund'rous storm
Had been off-shaken from his scatheless bark
He had heard distant years sweet concord yield,
And go to silence; having firmly kept
Majestical companionship with Time.
Anon his strength waxed proud: his tusky roots
Forced for themselves a path on every side,
Riving the earth; and, in their savage scorn,
Casting it from them like a thing unclean,
Which might impede his naked clambering
Unto the heavens. Now blasted, peeled, he stood.
By the gone night, whose lightning had come in
And rent him, even as it rent the man
Beneath his shade: and there the strong and weak
Communion joined in deathly agony.
There, underneath, I lent my feverish strength,
To scoop a lodgement for the traveller's corse.
I gave it to the silence and the pit,
And strewed the heavy earth on all: and then—
I—I, whose hands had formed that silent house,—
I could not look thereon, but turned and wept!

*   *   *

O Death—O crownèd Death—pale-steedèd Death!
Whose name doth make our respiration brief,
Muffling the spirit's drum! Thou, whom men know
Alone by charnel-houses, and the dark
Sweeping of funeral feathers, and the scath
Of happy days,—love deemed inviolate!

Thou of the shrouded face, which to have seen
Is to be very awful, like thyself!—
Thou, whom all flesh shall see!—thou, who dost call,
And there is none to answer!—thou, whose call
Changeth all beauty into what we fear,
Changeth all glory into what we tread,
Genius to silence, wrath to nothingness,
And love—not love!—thou hast no change for love!
Thou, who art Life's bethrothed, and bear'st her forth
To scare her with sad sights,—who hast thy joy
Where'er the peopled towns are dumb with plague,—
Where'er the battle and the vulture meet,—
Where'er the deep sea writhes like Laocoon
Beneath the serpent winds, and vessels split
On secret rocks, and men go gurgling down,
Down, down, to lose their shriekings in the depth!
O universal thou! who comest ay
Among the minstrels, and their tongue is tied;
Among the sophists, and their brain is still;
Among the mourners, and their wail is done;
Among the dancers, and their tinkling feet
No more make echoes on the tombing earth;
Among the wassail rout, and all the lamps
Are quenched, and withered the wine-pouring hands!
Mine heart is armèd not in panoply
Of the old Roman iron, nor assumes
The Stoic valour. 'Tis a human heart,
And so confesses, with a human fear;—
That only for the hope the cross inspires,
That only for the MAN who died and lives,
'Twould crouch beneath thy sceptre's royalty,
With faintness of the pulse, and backward cling
To life. But knowing what I soothly know,
High-seeming Death, I dare thee! and have hope,
In God's good time, of showing to thy face
An unsuccumbing spirit, which sublime

May cast away the low anxieties
That wait upon the flesh—the reptile moods;
And enter that eternity to come,
Where live the dead, and only Death shall die.

Poems Selected from

THE SERAPHIM,
AND OTHER POEMS
(1838)

Preface

In this volume—the first published under her own name —Elizabeth Barrett included thirty-six shorter poems with the long title poem (which was a lyrical drama on the subject of the Crucifixion). The range within them was wide. Most popular, with critics and public, were the ballads which reminded *The Atlas* critic of Tennyson. *The Metropolitan Magazine* called "The Romaunt of Margret" "all but perfect". Modern feminist criticism now sees these ballads as subversive—Professor Dorothy Mermin thinks "these poems add up to a thorough-going reassessment—often a total repudiation—of the Victorian ideas about womanliness". To the Victorians, these ballads were sweet and innocent; to Professor Mermin and others they were "exploring with a passionate heart and a very cold eye what was becoming her central subject: the psychological oppression of women . . ."

The lyrics in this volume were also popular. *Blackwood's* magazine, while conceding that "My Doves" was "unambitious", praised the poem because it would "live in the memory of many a gentle girl". Unmentioned in any review were the much more interesting lyric "A Sea-Side Walk" and "Man and Nature" which perfectly summed up Elizabeth Barrett's philosophy at the age of thirty-two. During the decade since her mother's death (in 1828) she had struggled hard to overcome her sense of hopelessness and only managed to do so by reaffirming her religious faith and her faith in nature as a healing power.

A TRUE DREAM*

(Dreamed at Sidmouth, 1833)

I had not an evil end in view,
    Tho' I trod the evil way;
And why I practised the magic art,
    My dream it did not say.

I unsealed the vial mystical,
    I outpoured the liquid thing,
And while the smoke came wreathing out,
    I stood unshuddering.

The smoke came wreathing, wreathing out,
    All mute, and dark, and slow,
Till its cloud was stained with a fleshly hue,
    And a fleshly form 'gan show.

Then paused the smoke—the fleshly form
    Looked steadfast in mine ee,
His beard was black as a thundercloud,
    But I trembled not to see.

I unsealed the vial mystical,
    I outpoured the liquid thing,
And while the smoke came wreathing out,
    I stood unshuddering.

The smoke came wreathing, wreathing out,
    All mute, and dark and slow,
Till its cloud was stained with a fleshly hue,
    And a fleshly form 'gan show.

Then paused the smoke—but the mortal form
    A garment swart did veil,
I looked on it with fixed heart,
    Yea—not a pulse did fail!

(*See Note on the Text)

[31]

I unsealed the vial mystical,
    I outpoured the liquid thing,
And while the smoke came wreathing out,
    I stood unshuddering.

The smoke came wreathing, wreathing out,
    And now it was faster and lighter,
And it bore on its folds the rainbow's hues,
    Heaven could not show them brighter.

Then paused the smoke, the rainbow's hues
    Did a childish face express—
The rose in the cheek, the blue in the eyne,
    The yellow in the tress.

The fair young child shook back her hair,
    And round me her arms did wreathe,
Her lips were hard and cold as stone,
    They sucked away my breath.

I cast her off as she clung to me,
    With hate and shuddering;
I brake the vials, and foresware
    The cursed, cursed thing.

Anon outspake a brother of mine—
    'Upon the pavement, see,
Besprent with noisome poison slime,
    Those twining serpents three.'

Anon outspake my wildered heart
    As I saw the serpent train—
'I have called up three existences
    I cannot quench again.

'Alas! with unholy company,
  My lifetime they will scathe;
They will hiss in the storm, and on sunny days
  Will gleam and thwart my path.'

Outspake that pitying brother of mine—
  'Now nay, my sister, nay,
I will pour on them oil of vitriol,
  And burn their lives away.'

'Now nay, my brother, torture not,
  Now hold thine hand, and spare.'
He poured on them oil of vitriol,
  And did not heed my prayer.

I saw the drops of torture fall;
  I heard the shriekings rise,
While the serpents writhed in agony
  Beneath my dreaming eyes.

And while they shrieked, and while they writhed,
  And inward and outward wound,
They waxed larger, and their wail
  Assumed a human sound.

And glared their eyes, and their slimy scales
  Were roundly and redly bright,
Most like the lidless sun, what time
  Thro' the mist he meets your sight.

And larger and larger they waxed still,
  And longer still and longer;
And they shrieked in their pain, 'Come, come to us,
  We are stronger, we are stronger.'

Upon the ground I laid mine head,
    And heard the wailing sound;
I did not wail, I did not writhe—
    I laid me on the ground.

And larger and larger they waxed still
    And longer still and longer;
And they shrieked in their pangs, 'Come, come to us,
    We are stronger, we are stronger.'

Then up I raised my burning brow,
    My quiv'ring arms on high;
I spake in prayer, and I named aloud
    The name of sanctity.

And as in my anguish I prayed and named
    Aloud the holy name,
The impious mocking serpent voice
    Did echo back the same.

And larger and larger they waxed still,
    And stronger still and longer!
And they shrieked in their pangs, 'Come, come to us,
    We are stronger, we are stronger.'

Then out from among them arose a form
    In shroud of death indued—
I fled from him with wings of wind,
    With whirlwinds he pursued.

*   *   *

I stood by a chamber door, and thought
    Within its gloom to hide;
I locked the door, and the while forgot
    That I stood on the outer side.

And the knell of mine heart was wildly tolled
    While I grasped still the key;
For I felt beside me the icy breath,
    And knew that *that* was *he*.

I heard these words, 'Whoe'er doth *taste*,
    Will *drink* the magic bowl;
So her body may do my mission here
    Companioned by her soul.'

Mine hand was cold as the key it held,
    Mine heart had an iron weight;
I saw a gleam, I heard a sound—
    The clock was striking eight.

MAN AND NATURE

A sad man on a summer day
Did look upon the earth and say—

'Purple cloud, the hill-top binding,
Folded hills, the valleys wind in,
Valleys, with fresh streams among you,
Streams, with bosky trees along you,
Trees, with many birds and blossoms,
Birds, with music-trembling bosoms,
Blossoms, dropping dews that wreathe you
To your fellow flowers beneath you,
Flowers, that constellate on earth,
Earth, that shakest to the mirth
Of the merry Titan ocean,
All his shining hair in motion!
Why am I thus the only one
Who can be dark beneath the sun?'

[35]

But when the summer day was past,
He looked to heaven and smiled at last,
Self-answered so—

               'Because, O cloud,
Pressing with thy crumpled shroud
Heavily on mountain top,—
Hills, that almost seem to drop
Stricken with a misty death
To the valleys underneath,—
Valleys, sighing with the torrent,—
Waters, streaked with branches horrent,—
Branchless trees, that shake your head
Wildly o'er your blossoms spread
Where the common flowers are found,—
Flowers, with foreheads to the ground,—
Ground, that shriekest while the sea
With his iron smiteth thee—
I am, besides, the only one
Who can be bright *without* the sun.'

THE DESERTED GARDEN

I mind me in the days departed,
How often underneath the sun
With childish bounds I used to run
    To a garden long deserted.

The beds and walks were vanished quite;
And wheresoe'er had struck the spade,
The greenest grasses Nature laid,
    To sanctify her right.

I called the place my wilderness,
For no one entered there but I;
The sheep looked in, the grass to espy,
    And passed it ne'ertheless.

The trees were interwoven wild,
And spread their boughs enough about
To keep both sheep and shepherd out,
    But not a happy child.

Adventurous joy it was for me!
I crept beneath the boughs, and found
A circle smooth of mossy ground
    Beneath a poplar tree.

Old garden rose-trees hedged it in,
Bedropt with roses waxen-white
Well satisfied with dew and light
    And careless to be seen.

Long years ago it might befall,
When all the garden flowers were trim,
The grave old gardener prided him
    On these the most of all.

Some lady, stately overmuch,
Here moving with a silken noise,
Has blushed beside them at the voice
    That likened her to such.

And these, to make a diadem,
She often may have plucked and twined,
Half-smiling as it came to mind
    That few would look at *them*.

Oh, little thought that lady proud,
A child would watch her fair white rose,
When buried lay her whiter brows,
    And silk was changed for shroud!—

Nor thought that gardener (full of scorns
For men unlearned and simple phrase),
A child would bring it all its praise
    By creeping through the thorns!

To me upon my low moss seat,
Though never a dream the roses sent
Of science or love's compliment,
    I ween they smelt as sweet.

It did not move my grief to see
The trace of human step departed:
Because the garden was deserted,
    The blither place for me!

Friends, blame me not! a narrow ken
Has childhood 'twixt the sun and sward:
We draw the moral afterward—
    We feel the gladness then.

And gladdest hours for me did glide
In silence at the rose-tree wall;
A thrush made gladness musical
    Upon the other side.

Nor he nor I did e'er incline
To peck or pluck the blossom white;
How should I know but roses might
    Lead lives as glad as mine?

To make my hermit-home complete,
I brought clear water from the spring
Praised in its own low murmuring,—
    And cresses glossy wet.

And so, I thought, my likeness grew
(Without the melancholy tale)
To 'gentle hermit of the dale,'
    And Angelina too.

For oft I read within my nook
Such minstrel stories; till the breeze
Made sounds poetic in the trees,—
    And then I shut the book.

If I shut this wherein I write
I hear no more the wind athwart
Those trees,—nor feel that childish heart
    Delighting in delight.

My childhood from my life is parted,
My footstep from the moss which drew
Its fairy circle round: anew
    The garden is deserted.

Another thrush may there rehearse
The madrigals which sweetest are;
No more for me!—myself afar
    Do sing a sadder verse.

Ah me, ah me! when erst I lay
In that child's-nest so greenly wrought,
I laughed unto myself and thought
    'The time will pass away.'

And still I laughed, and did not fear
But that, whene'er was past away
The childish time, some happier play
   My womanhood would cheer.

I knew the time would pass away,
And yet, beside the rose-tree wall,
Dear God, how seldom, if at all,
   Did I look up to pray!

The time is past;—and now that grows
The cypress high among the trees,
And I behold white sepulchres
   As well as the white rose,—

When graver, meeker thoughts are given,
And I have learnt to lift my face,
Reminded how earth's greenest place
   The colour draws from heaven,—

It something saith for earthly pain,
But more for Heavenly promise free,
That I who was, would shrink to be
   That happy child again.

THE SEA-MEW

I

How joyously the young sea-mew
Lay dreaming on the waters blue
Whereon our little bark had thrown
A little shade, the only one,
But shadows ever man pursue.

II

Familiar with the waves and free
As if their own white foam were he,
His heart upon the heart of ocean
Lay learning all its mystic motion,
And throbbing to the throbbing sea.

III

And such a brightness in his eye
As if the ocean and the sky
Within him had lit up and nurst
A soul God gave him not at first,
To comprehend their majesty.

IV

We were not cruel, yet did sunder
His white wing from the blue waves under,
And bound it, while his fearless eyes
Shone up to ours in calm surprise,
As deeming us some ocean wonder.

V

We bore our ocean bird unto
A grassy place where he might view
The flowers that curtsey to the bees,
The waving of the tall green trees,
The falling of the silver dew.

VI

But flowers of earth were pale to him
Who had seen the rainbow fishes swim;
And when earth's dew around him lay
He thought of ocean's wingèd spray,
And his eye waxèd sad and dim.

VII

The green trees round him only made
A prison with their darksome shade;
And drooped his wing, and mournëd he
For his own boundless glittering sea—
Albeit he knew not they could fade.

VIII

Then One her gladsome face did bring,
Her gentle voice's murmuring,
In ocean's stead his heart to move
And teach him what was human love:
He thought it a strange mournful thing.

IX

He lay down in his grief to die,
(First looking to the sea-like sky
That hath no waves) because, alas!
Our human touch did on him pass,
And with our touch, our agony.

A SEA-SIDE WALK

I

We walked beside the sea
After a day which perished silently
Of its own glory—like the princess weird,
Who, combating the Genius, scorched and seared,
Uttered with burning breath, 'Ho! victory!'
And sank adown, an heap of ashes pale:
    So runs the Arab tale.

II

The sky above us showed
A universal and unmoving cloud,
On which the cliffs permitted us to see
Only the outline of their majesty,
As master-minds, when gazed at by the crowd!
And shining with a gloom, the water gray
    Swang in its moon-taught way.

III

Nor moon, nor stars were out:
They did not dare to tread so soon about,
Though trembling, in the footsteps of the sun;
The light was neither night's nor day's, but one
Which, life-like, had a beauty in its doubt,
And Silence's impassioned breathings round
    Seemed wandering into sound.

IV

O solemn-beating heart
Of nature! I have knowledge that thou art
Bound unto man's by cords he cannot sever—
And, what time they are slackened by him ever,
So to attest his own supernal part,
Still runneth thy vibration fast and strong
    The slackened cord along:

V

For though we never spoke
Of the gray water and the shaded rock,
Dark wave and stone unconsciously were fused
Into the plaintive speaking that we used
Of absent friends and memories unforsook;
And, had we seen each other's face, we had
    Seen haply each was sad.

MY DOVES

O Weisheit! Du red'st wie eine Taube!
GOETHE

My little doves have left a nest
   Upon an Indian tree,
Whose leaves fantastic take their rest
   Or motion from the sea;
For, ever there, the sea-winds go
With sunlit paces to and fro.

The tropic flowers looked up to it,
   The tropic stars looked down,
And there my little doves did sit,
   With feathers softly brown,
And glittering eyes that showed their right
To general Nature's deep delight.

And God them taught, at every close
   Of murmuring waves beyond,
And green leaves round, to interpose
   Their choral voices fond,
Interpreting that love must be
The meaning of the earth and sea.

Fit ministers! Of living loves,
   Theirs hath the calmest fashion,
Their living voice the likest moves
   To lifeless intonation.
The lovely monotone of springs
And winds, and such insensate things.

My little doves were ta'en away
    From that glad nest of theirs,
Across an ocean rolling grey,
    And tempest-clouded airs:
My little doves,—who lately knew
The sky and wave by warmth and blue!

And now, within the city prison,
    In mist and chillness pent,
With sudden upward look they listen
    For sounds of past content—
For lapse of water, swell of breeze,
Or nut-fruit falling from the trees.

The stir without the glow of passion,
    The triumph of the mart,
The gold and silver as they clash on
    Man's cold metallic heart—
The roar of wheels, the cry for bread,—
These only sounds are heard instead.

Yet still, as on my human hand
    Their fearless heads they lean,
And almost seem to understand
    What human musings mean,
(Their eyes, with such a plaintive shine,
Are fastened upwardly to mine!)

Soft falls their chant as on the nest
    Beneath the sunny zone;
For love that stirred it in their breast
    Has not aweary grown,
And 'neath the city's shade can keep
The well of music clear and deep.

And love that keeps the music, fills
　　With pastoral memories:
All echoings from out the hills,
　　All droppings from the skies,
All flowings from the wave and wind,
Remembered in their chant, I find.

So teach ye me the wisest part,
　　My little doves! to move
Along the city-ways with heart
　　Assured by holy love,
And vocal with such songs as own
A fountain to the world unknown.

'Twas hard to sing by Babel's stream—
　　More hard, in Babel's street!
But if the soulless creatures deem
　　Their music not unmeet
For sunless walls—let *us* begin,
Who wear immortal wings within!

To me, fair memories belong
　　Of scenes that used to bless,
For no regret, but present song,
　　And lasting thankfulness,
And very soon to break away,
Like types, in purer things than they.

I will have hopes that cannot fade,
　　For flowers the valley yields!
I will have humble thoughts instead
　　Of silent, dewy fields!
My spirit and my God shall be
My seaward hill, my boundless sea.

NIGHT AND THE MERRY MAN

NIGHT

'Neath my moon what doest thou.
With a somewhat paler brow
Than she giveth to the ocean?
He, without a pulse or motion,
Muttering low before her stands,
Lifting his invoking hands,
Like a seer before a sprite,
To catch her oracles of light.
But thy soul out-trembles now
Many pulses on thy brow!
Where be all thy laughters clear,
Others laughed alone to hear?

Where, thy quaint jests, said for fame?
Where, thy dances, mixed with game?
Where, thy festive companies,
Moonèd o'er with ladies' eyes,
All more bright for thee, I trow?
'Neath my moon, what doest thou?

THE MERRY MAN

I am digging my warm heart,
Till I find its coldest part;
I am digging wide and low,
Further than a spade will go;
Till that, when the pit is deep
And large enough, I there may heap
All my present pain and past
Joy, dead things that look aghast
By the daylight.—Now 'tis done.
Throw them in, by one and one!
I must laugh, at rising sun.

Memories—of fancy's golden
Treasures which my hands have holden,
Till the chillness made them ache;
Of childhood's hopes, that used to wake
If birds were in a singing strain,
And for less cause, sleep again;
Of the moss-seat in the wood,
Where I trysted solitude;
Of the hill-top, where the wind
Used to follow me behind,
Then in sudden rush to blind
Both my glad eyes with my hair
Taken gladly in the snare;
Of the climbing up the rocks,—
Of the playing 'neath the oaks,
Which retain beneath them now
Only shadow of the bough;
Of the lying on the grass
While the clouds did overpass,
Only they, so lightly driven,
Seeming betwixt me and Heaven!
Of the little prayers serene,
Murmuring of earth and sin;
Of large-leaved philosophy
Leaning from my childish knee;
Of poetic book sublime,
Soul-kissed for the first dear time,—
Greek or English,—ere I knew
Life was not a poem too.
Throw them in, by one and one!
I must laugh, at rising sun.
Of the glorious ambitions,
Yet unquenched by their fruitions;
Of the reading out the nights;
Of the straining at mad heights;
Of achievements, less descried

By a dear few, than magnified;
Of praises, from the many earned,
When praise from love was undiscerned;
Of the sweet reflecting gladness,
Softened by itself to sadness—
Throw them in, by one and one!
I must laugh, at rising sun.

What are these? more, more than these!
Throw in, dearer memories!—
Of voices—whereof but to speak,
Makes mine own all sunk and weak;
Of smiles, the thought of which is sweeping
All my soul to floods of weeping;
Of looks, whose absence fain would weigh
My looks to the ground for ay;
Of clasping hands—ah me! I wring
Mine, and in a tremble fling
Downward, downward, all this paining!
Partings, with the sting remaining;
Meetings, with a deeper throe,
Since the joy is ruined so;
Changes, with a fiery burning—
(Shadows upon all the turning);
Thoughts of—with a storm they came—
Them, I have not breath to name.
Downward, downward, be they cast
In the pit! and now at last
My work beneath the moon is done,
And I shall laugh, at rising sun.

But let me pause or ere I cover
All my treasures darkly over.
I will speak not in thine ears,
Only tell my beaded tears
Silently, most silently!

[49]

When the last is calmly told,
Let that same moist rosary
With the rest sepùlchred be.
Finished now. The darksome mould
Sealeth up the darksome pit.
I will lay no stone on it:
Grasses I will sow instead,
Fit for Queen Titania's tread;
Flowers, encoloured with the sun,
And αι αι written upon none.
Thus, whenever saileth by
The Lady World of dainty eye,
Not a grief shall here remain,
Silken shoon to damp or stain;
And while she lisps, 'I have not seen
Any place more smooth and clean' . . .
Here she cometh!—Ha, ha!—who
Laughs as loud as I can do?

THE SLEEP

I

Of all the thoughts of God that are
Borne inward into souls afar,
Along the Psalmist's music deep,
Now tell me if that any is,
For gift or grace surpassing this—
'He giveth His belovèd, sleep?'

II

What would we give to our beloved?
The hero's heart to be unmoved,
The poet's star-tuned harp to sweep,
The patriot's voice to teach and rouse,
The monarch's crown to light the brows?—
He giveth His belovèd, sleep.

III

What do we give to our beloved?
A little faith all undisproved,
A little dust to overweep,
And bitter memories to make
The whole earth blasted for our sake:
He giveth His belovèd, sleep.

IV

'Sleep soft, beloved!' we sometimes say,
Who have no tune to charm away
Sad dreams that through the eyelids creep.
But never doleful dream again
Shall break the happy slumber when
He giveth his belovèd, sleep.

V

O earth, so full of dreary noises!
O men, with wailing in your voices!
O delvèd gold, the wailers heap!
Of strife, O curse, that o'er it fall!
God strikes a silence through you all,
And giveth His belovèd, sleep.

VI

His dews drop mutely on the hill;
His cloud above it saileth still,
Though on its slope men sow and reap.
More softly than the dew is shed,
Or cloud is floated overhead,
He giveth His belovèd, sleep.

VII

Aye, men may wonder while they scan
A living, thinking, feeling man
Confirmed in such a rest to keep;
But angels say, and through the word
I think their happy smile is *heard*—
'He giveth His belovèd, sleep.'

VIII

For me, my heart that erst did go
Most like a tired child at a show,
That sees through tears the mummers leap,
Would now its wearied vision close,
Would childlike on His love repose
Who giveth His belovèd, sleep.

IX

And friends, dear friends, when it shall be
That this low breath is gone from me,
And round my bier ye come to weep,
Let One, most loving of you all,
Say, 'Not a tear must o'er her fall!
'He giveth His belovèd sleep.'

THE ROMAUNT OF MARGRET

Can my affections find out nothing best,
But still and still remove?
QUARLES

I

I plant a tree whose leaf
    The yew-tree leaf will suit;
But when its shade is o'er you laid,
    Turn round and pluck the fruit.
Now reach my harp from off the wall
    Where shines the sun aslant!
The sun may shine and we be cold—
O hearken, loving hearts and bold,
    Unto my wild romaunt,
                            Margret, Margret.

II

Sitteth the fair ladye
    Close to the river side,
Which runneth on with a merry tone
    Her merry thoughts to guide.
It runneth through the trees,
    It runneth by the hill,
Nathless the lady's thoughts have found
    A way more pleasant still.
                            Margret, Margret.

III

The night is in her hair
    And giveth shade to shade,
And the pale moonlight on her forehead white
    Like a spirit's hand is laid;
Her lips part with a smile
    Instead of speakings done:
I ween, she thinketh of a voice,
    Albeit uttering none.
                    Margret, Margret.

IV

All little birds do sit
    With heads beneath their wings:
Nature doth seem in a mystic dream,
    Absorbed from her living things.
That dream by that ladye
    Is certes unpartook,
For she looketh to the high cold stars
    With a tender human look.
                    Margret, Margret.

V

The lady's shadow lies
    Upon the running river;
It lieth no less in its quietness,
    For that which resteth never:
Most like a trusting heart
    Upon a passing faith,—
Or as, upon the course of life,
    The steadfast doom of death.
                    Margret, Margret.

The lady doth not move,
    The lady doth not dream,
Yet she seeth her shade no longer laid
    In rest upon the stream.
It shaketh without wind,
    It parteth from the tide,
It standeth upright in the cleft moonlight,
    It sitteth at her side.
                    Margret, Margret.

VII

Look in its face, ladye,
    And keep thee from thy swound!
With a spirit bold, thy pulses hold,
    And hear its voice's sound.
For so will sound thy voice,
    When thy face is to the wall;
And such will be thy face, ladye,
    When the maidens work thy pall.
                    Margret, Margret.

'Am I not like to thee?'—
    The voice was calm and low;
And between each word you might have heard
    The silent forests grow.
'*The like may sway the like,*'
    By which mysterious law
Mine eyes from thine and my lips from thine
    The light and breath may draw.
                    Margret, Margret.

'My lips do need thy breath,
    My lips do need thy smile,
And my pallid eyne, that light in thine
    Which met the stars erewhile.
Yet go with light and life,
    If that thou lovest one
In all the earth, who loveth thee
    As truly as the sun,
                    Margret, Margret.'

X

Her cheek had waxèd white
    Like cloud at fall of snow;
Then like to one at set of sun
    It waxèd red alsò;
For love's name maketh bold,
    As if the loved were near.
And then she sighed the deep long sigh
    Which cometh after fear.
                    Margret, Margret.

XI

'Now sooth, I fear thee not—
    Shall never fear thee now!'
(And a noble sight was the sudden light
    Which lit her lifted brow.)
'Can earth be dry of streams?
    Or hearts, of love?' she said;
'Who doubteth love, can know not love:
    He is already dead.'
                    Margret, Margret.

XII

'I have' . . . and here her lips
  Some words in pause did keep,
And gave the while a quiet smile,
  As if they paused in sleep,—
'I have . . . a brother dear,
  A knight of knightly fame!
I broidered him a knightly scarf
  With letters of my name.
                    Margret, Margret.

XIII

'I fed his grey goss-hawk,
  I kissed his fierce bloodhound,
I sate at home when he might come
  And caught his horn's far sound:
I sang him hunters' songs,
  I poured him the red wine—
He looked across the cup and said,
  I love thee, sister mine.'
                    Margret, Margret.

XIV

IT trembled on the grass,
  With a low, shadowy laughter;
The sounding river which rolled for ever,
  Stood dumb and stagnant after.
'Brave knight thy brother is!
  But better loveth he
Thy chaliced wine than thy chanted song,
  And better both, than thee,
                    Margret, Margret.'

The lady did not heed
    The river's silence while
Her own thoughts still ran at their will,
    And calm was still her smile.
    'My little sister wears
      The look our mother wore:
I smooth her locks with a golden comb,
    I bless her evermore.'

              Margret, Margret.

'I gave her my first bird,
    When first my voice it knew;
I made her share my posies rare,
    And told her where they grew.
    I taught her God's dear name
      With prayer and praise, to tell—
She looked from heaven into my face,
    And said, *I love thee well*.'

              Margret, Margret.

XVII

IT trembled on the grass
    With a low, shadowy laughter:
You could see each bird as it woke and stared
    Through the shrivelled foliage after.
    'Fair child thy sister is!
      But better loveth she
Thy golden comb than thy gathered flowers,
    And better both, than thee,

              Margret, Margret.'

XVIII

The lady did not heed
    The withering on the bough:
Still calm her smile, albeit the while
    A little pale her brow.
  'I have a father old,
    The lord of ancient halls;
An hundred friends are in his court,
    Yet only me he calls.
                        Margret, Margret.

XIX

'An hundred knights are in his court,
    Yet read I by his knee;
And when forth they go to the tourney show,
    I rise not up to see.
  'Tis a weary book to read,
    My tryst's at set of sun,
But loving and dear beneath the stars
    Is his blessing when I've done.'
                        Margret, Margret.

XX

IT trembled on the grass
    With a low, shadowy laughter;
And moon and star, though bright and far,
    Did shrink and darken after.
  'High lord thy father is!
    But better loveth he
His ancient halls than his hundred friends,
    His ancient halls, than thee,
                        Margret, Margret.'

XXI

The lady did not heed
    That the far stars did fail:
Still calm her smile, albeit the while . . .
    Nay, but she is not pale!
'I have a more than friend
    Across the mountains dim:
No other's voice is soft to me,
    Unless it nameth *him*.'
                  Margret, Margret.

XXII

'Though louder beats mine heart
    I know his tread again,
And his far plume ay, unless turned away,
    For the tears do blind me then.
We brake no gold, a sign
    Of stronger faith to be,—
But I wear his last look in my soul,
    Which said, *I love but thee!*'
                  Margret, Margret.

XXIII

IT trembled on the grass
    With a low, shadowy laughter;
And the wind did toll, as a passing soul
    Were sped by church-bell after;
And shadows, 'stead of light,
    Fell from the stars above,
In flakes of darkness on her face
    Still bright with trusting love.
                  Margret, Margret.

XXIV

'He *loved* but only thee!
    That love is transient too:
The wild hawk's bill doth dabble still
    I' the mouth that vowed thee true.
Will he open his dull eyes,
    When tears fall on his brow?
Behold, the death-worm to his heart
    Is a nearer thing than *thou*,
                Margret, Margret.'

Her face was on the ground—
    None saw the agony,
But the men at sea did that night agree
    They heard a drowning cry;
And when the morning brake,
    Fast rolled the river's tide,
With the green trees waving overhead,
    And a white corse laid beside.
              Margret, Margret.

A knight's bloodhound and he
    The funeral watch did keep;
With a thought o' the chase he stroked its face
    As it howled to see him weep.
A fair child kissed the dead,
    But shrank before its cold;
And alone yet proudly in his hall
    Did stand a baron old.
              Margret, Margret.

Hang up my harp again!
    I have no voice for song:
Not song, but wail, and mourners pale,
    Not bards, to love belong.
    O failing human love!
        O light, by darkness known!
O false, the while thou treadest earth!
        O deaf beneath the stone!
                        Margret, Margret.

A ROMANCE OF THE GANGES

I

Seven maidens 'neath the midnight
    Stand near the river-sea.
Whose water sweepeth white around
    The shadow of the tree.
The moon and earth are face to face,
    And earth is slumbering deep;
The wave-voice seems the voice of dreams
    That wander through her sleep.
                    The river floweth on.

II

What bring they 'neath the midnight,
    Beside the river-sea?
They bring the human heart wherein
    No nightly calm can be,—
That droppeth never with the wind,
    Nor drieth with the dew:
Oh, calm it, God! Thy calm is broad
    To cover spirits, too.
                    The river floweth on.

III

The maidens lean them over
  The waters, side by side,
And shun each other's deepening eyes,
  And gaze adown the tide;
For each within a little boat
  A little lamp hath put,
And heaped for freight some lily's weight
  Or scarlet rose half shut.
                    The river floweth on.

IV

Of shell of coco carven,
  Each little boat is made:
Each carries a lamp, and carries a flower,
  And carries a hope unsaid;
And when the boat hath carried the lamp
  Unquenched, till out of sight,
The maiden is sure that love will endure,—
  But love will fail with light.
                    The river floweth on.

V

Why, all the stars are ready
  To symbolize the soul,
The stars untroubled by the wind,
  Unwearied as they roll;
And yet the soul by instinct sad
  Reverts to symbols low—
To that small flame, whose very name
  Breathed o'er it, shakes it so!
                    The river floweth on.

VI

Six boats are on the river,
  Seven maidens on the shore,
While still above them steadfastly
  The stars shine evermore.
Go, little boats, go soft and safe,
  And guard the symbol spark!—
The boats aright go safe and bright
  Across the waters dark.
                    The river floweth on.

VII

The maiden Luti watcheth
  Where onwardly they float:
That look in her dilating eyes
  Might seem to drive her boat!
Her eyes still mark the constant fire,
  And kindling unawares
That hopeful while, she lets a smile
  Creep silent through her prayers.
                    The river floweth on.

VIII

The smile—where hath it wandered?
  She riseth from her knee,
She holds her dark, wet locks away—
  There is no light to see!
She cries a quick and bitter cry—
  'Nuleeni, launch me thine!
We must have light abroad to-night,
  For all the wreck of mine.'
                    The river floweth on.

IX

'I do remember watching
   Beside this river-bed,
When on my childish knee was laid
   My dying father's head;
I turned mine own, to keep the tears
   From falling on his face:
What doth it prove when Death and Love
   Choose out the self-same place?'
                The river floweth on.

X

'They say the dead are joyful
   The death-change here receiving:
Who say—ah, me!—who dare to say
   Where joy comes to the living?
Thy boat, Nuleeni! look not sad—
   Light up the waters rather!
I weep no faithless lover where
   I wept a loving father.'
                The river floweth on.

XI

'My heart foretold his falsehood
   Eere my little boat grew dim:
And though I closed mine eyes to dream
   That one last dream of *him*,
They shall not now be wet to see
   The shining vision go:
From earth's cold love I look above
   To the holy house of snow.'
                The river floweth on.

XII

'Come thou—thou never knewest
    A grief, that thou shouldst fear one!
Thou wearest still the happy look
    That shines beneath a dear one;
Thy humming-bird is in the sun,
    Thy cuckoo in the grove,
And all the three broad worlds, for thee
    Are full of wandering love.'
                  The river floweth on.

XIII

'Why, maiden, dost thou loiter?
    What secret wouldst thou cover?
That peepul cannot hide thy boat,
    And I can guess thy lover.
I heard thee sob his name in sleep . . .
    It was a name I knew;
Come, little maid, be not afraid,
    But let us prove him true!'
                  The river floweth on.

XIV

The little maiden cometh,
    She cometh shy and slow,
I ween she seeth through her lids,
    They drop adown so low;
Her tresses meet her small bare feet—
    She stands and speaketh nought,
Yet blusheth red, as if she said
    The name she only thought.
                  The river floweth on.

XV

She knelt beside the water,
   She lighted up the flame,
And o'er her youthful forehead's calm
   The fitful radiance came:—
'Go, little boat, go, soft and safe,
   And guard the symbol spark!'
Soft, safe, doth float the little boat
   Across the waters dark.
                  The river floweth on.

XVI

Glad tears her eyes have blinded,
   The light they cannot reach;
She turneth with that sudden smile
   She learnt before her speech—
'I do not hear his voice! the tears
   Have dimmed my light away!
But the symbol light will last to-night,
   The love will last for ay.'
                  The river floweth on.

XVII

Then Luti spake behind her,
   Outspake she bitterly,
'By the symbol light that lasts to-night,
   Wilt vow a vow to me?'—
Nuleeni gazeth up her face,
   Soft answer maketh she:
'By loves that last when lights are past,
   I vow that vow to thee!'
                  The river floweth on.

XVIII

An earthly look had Luti
   Though her voice was deep as prayer:
'The rice is gathered from the plains
   To cast upon thine hair.
But when *he* comes, his marriage-band
   Around thy neck to throw,
Thy bride-smile raise to meet his gaze,
And whisper,—*There is one betrays,*
   While Luti suffers woe.'
                                    The river floweth on.

XIX

'And when in seasons after,
   Thy little bright-faced son
Shall lean against thy knee and ask
   What deeds his sire hath done,
Press deeper down thy mother-smile
   His glossy curls among—
View deep his pretty childish eyes,
And whisper,—*There is none denies,*
   While Luti speaks of wrong.'
                                    The river floweth on.

XX

Nuleeni looked in wonder,
    Yet softly answered she:
'By loves that last when lights are past,
    I vowed that vow to thee.
But why glads it thee that a bride-day be
    By a word of *woe* defiled?
That a word of *wrong* take the cradle-song
    From the ear of a sinless child?'—
'Why?' Luti said, and her laugh was dread,
    And her eyes dilated wild—
'That the fair new love may her bridegroom prove,
    And the father shame the child.'
                The river floweth on.

XXI

'Thou flowest still, O river,
    Thou flowest 'neath the moon!
Thy lily hath not changed a leaf,
    Thy charmèd lute a tune!
He mixed his voice with thine—and *his*
    Was all I heard around;
But now, beside his chosen bride,
    I hear the river's sound.'
                The river floweth on.

'I gaze upon her beauty
  Through the tresses that enwreathe it;
The light above thy wave, is hers—
  My rest, alone beneath it.
Oh, give me back the dying look
  My father gave thy water!
Give back!—and let a little love
  O'erwatch his weary daughter!'
                The river floweth on.

'Give back!' she hath departed—
  The word is wandering with her;
And the stricken maidens hear afar
  The step and cry together.
Frail symbols? None are frail enow
  For mortal joys to borrow!—
While bright doth float Nuleeni's boat,
  She weepeth, dark with sorrow.
                The river floweth on.

Poems Selected from

POEMS

2 volumes

(1844)

Preface

It is difficult to find a poem in this collection which does not deal with the theme of death or use the vocabulary and trappings of death. Several fine sonnets, for instance, form a sequence on the subject of grief, and they show Elizabeth Barrett attempting to make sense of the suffering which death causes.

The poem most often singled out for praise was "Lady Geraldine's Courtship" (it was in this poem that Elizabeth Barrett flattered Robert Browning and precipitated their correspondence). It was read as an enjoyable story, and no one pointed out how unusual it was that the heroine, a rich and powerful woman, controls the fate of her lover instead of the other way round. The success of this poem—finished in a hurry to make up a full volume—astounded its author. She was encouraged to begin contemplating another such poem "comprehending the aspect and manners of modern life"—the first reference to *Aurora Leigh*, not begun for another ten years.

There was a growing concern with how women were treated in society in many of the poems. "The Lady's Yes" expresses disgust at how courtships are conducted: "Bertha in the Lane" condemns the fickle nature of men's love; and "Loved Once" despises all love that is not eternal. All passed without comment, except to be labelled "morbid". Much more to everyone's taste was "Catarina to Camoens", which was also one of Robert Browning's favourite.

"The Cry of the Children" also met with general approval. Critics did not think women should attempt political poetry (*Blackwood's* said that when women discussed politics they "overstepped the pale of propriety") but it was by then perfectly acceptable for them to describe social evils and weep over them. Elizabeth had read the Parliamentary Reports on conditions in factories because her friend R. H. Horne was one of the investigating team. She was gratified by the success of this poem which, like the praise for "Lady Geraldine's Courtship", encouraged her to go in the direction she was already contemplating: towards representing the ills of her age and "speaking out".

DE PROFUNDIS*

I

The face which, duly as the sun,
Rose up for me with life begun,
To mark all bright hours of the day
With hourly love, is dimmed away,—
And yet my days go on, go on.

II

The tongue which, like a stream, could run
Smooth music from the roughest stone,
And every morning with 'Good day'
Make each day good, is hushed away,—
And yet my days go on, go on.

III

The heart which, like a staff, was one
For mine to lean and rest upon,
The strongest on the longest day
With steadfast love, is caught away,—
And yet my days go on, go on.

IV

And cold before my summer's done,
And deaf in Nature's general tune,
And fallen too low for special fear,
And here, with hope no longer here,—
While the tears drop, my days go on.

V

The world goes whispering to its own,
'This anguish pierces to the bone';
And tender friends go sighing round,
'What love can ever cure this wound?'
My days go on, my days go on.

(*See Note on the Text)

VI

The past rolls forward on the sun
And makes all night. O dreams begun,
Not to be ended! Ended bliss,
And life that will not end in this!
My days go on, my days go on.

VII

Breath freezes on my lips to moan:
As one alone, once not alone,
I sit and knock at Nature's door,
Heart-bare, heart-hungry, very poor,
Whose desolated days go on.

VIII

I knock and cry,—Undone, undone!
Is there no help, no comfort,—none?
No gleaning in the wide wheat-plains
Where others drive their loaded wains?
My vacant days go on, go on.

IX

This Nature, though the snows be down,
Thinks kindly of the bird of June:
The little red hip on the tree
Is ripe for such. What is for me,
Whose days so winterly go on?

X

No bird am I, to sing in June,
And dare not ask an equal boon.
Good nests and berries red are Nature's
To give away to better creatures,—
And yet my days go on, go on.

I ask less kindness to be done,—
Only to loose these pilgrim-shoon
(Too early worn and grimed), with sweet
Cool deathly touch to these tired feet,
Till days go out which now go on.

Only to lift the turf unmown
From off the earth where it has grown,
Some cubit-space, and say, 'Behold,
Creep in, poor Heart, beneath that fold,
Forgetting how the days go on.'

What harm would that do? Green anon
The sward would quicken, overshone
By skies as blue; and crickets might
Have leave to chirp there day and night
While my new rest went on, went on.

From gracious Nature have I won
Such liberal bounty? may I run
So, lizard-like, within her side,
And there be safe, who now am tried
By days that painfully go on?

—A Voice reproves me thereupon,
More sweet than Nature's when the drone
Of bees is sweetest, and more deep
Than when the rivers overleap
The shuddering pines, and thunder on.

XVI

God's Voice, not Nature's! Night and noon
He sits upon the great white throne
And listens for the creatures' praise.
What babble we of days and days?
The Dayspring He, whose days go on.

XVII

He reigns above, He reigns alone;
Systems burn out and leave His throne:
Fair mists of seraphs melt and fall
Around Him, changeless amid all,—
Ancient of Days, whose days go on.

XVIII

He reigns below, He reigns alone,
And, having life in love forgone
Beneath the crown of sovran thorns,
He reigns the Jealous God. Who mourns
Or rules with Him, while days go on?

XIX

By anguish which made pale the sun,
I hear Him charge His saints that none
Among His creatures anywhere
Blaspheme against Him with despair,
However darkly days go on.

XX

Take from my head the thorn-wreath brown!
No mortal grief deserves that crown.
O súpreme Love, chief Misery,
The sharp regalia are for THEE
Whose days eternally go on!

XXI

For us,—whatever's undergone,
Thou knowest, willest what is done.
Grief may be joy misunderstood;
Only the Good discerns the good.
I trust Thee while my days go on.

XXII

Whatever's lost, it first was won:
We will not struggle nor impugn.
Perhaps the cup was broken here,
That Heaven's new wine might show more clear.
I praise Thee while my days go on.

XXIII

I praise Thee while my days go on;
I love Thee while my days go on:
Through dark and dearth, through fire and frost,
With emptied arms and treasure lost,
I thank Thee while my days go on.

XXIV

And having in Thy life-depth thrown
Being and suffering (which are one),
As a child drops his pebble small
Down some deep well, and hears it fall
Smiling—so I. THY DAYS GO ON.

PAST AND FUTURE

My future will not copy fair my past
On any leaf but Heaven's. Be fully done,
Supernal Will! I would not fain be one
Who, satisfying thirst and breaking fast
Upon the fullness of the heart, at last
Says no grace after meat. My wine has run
Indeed out of my cup, and there is none
To gather up the bread of my repast
Scattered and trampled,—yet I find some good
In earth's green herbs, and streams that bubble up
Clear from the darkling ground,—content until
I sit with angels before better food.
Dear Christ! when Thy new vintage fills my cup,
This hand shall shake no more, nor that wine spill.

GRIEF

I tell you, hopeless grief is passionless;
That only men incredulous of despair,
Half-taught in anguish, through the midnight air
Beat upward to God's throne in loud access
Of shrieking and reproach. Full desertness
In souls, as countries, lieth silent-bare
Under the blanching, vertical eye-glare
Of the absolute Heavens. Deep-hearted man, express
Grief for thy Dead in silence like to death:—
Most like a monumental statue set
In everlasting watch and moveless woe,
Till itself crumble to the dust beneath.
Touch it: the marble eyelids are not wet;
If it could weep, it could arise and go.

[79]

TEARS

Thank God, bless God, all ye who suffer not
More grief than ye can weep for. That is well—
That is light grieving! lighter, none befell
Since Adam forfeited the primal lot.
Tears! what are tears? The babe weeps in its cot,
The mother singing,—at her marriage-bell
The bride weeps,—and before the oracle
Of high-faned hills, the poet has forgot
Such moisture on his cheeks. Thank God for grace,
Ye who weep only! If, as some have done,
Ye grope tear-blinded in a desert place
And touch but tombs,—look up! those tears will run
Soon in long rivers down the lifted face,
And leave the vision clear for stars and sun.

SUBSTITUTION

When some beloved voice that was to you
Both sound and sweetness, faileth suddenly,
And silence against which you dare not cry,
Aches round you like a strong disease and new—
What hope? what help? what music will undo
That silence to your sense? Not friendship's sigh—
Not reason's subtle count; not melody
Of viols, nor of pipes that Faunus blew.
Not songs of poets, nor of nightingales
Whose hearts leap upward through the cypress-trees
To the clear moon! nor yet the spheric laws
Self-chanted,—nor the angels' sweet All hails,
Met in the smile of God: nay, none of these.
Speak THOU, availing Christ!—and fill this pause.

[80]

LADY GERALDINE'S COURTSHIP

A ROMANCE OF THE AGE

A poet writes to his friend.
PLACE—*A room in Wycombe Hall.*
TIME—*Late in the evening.*

Dear my friend and fellow student,
    I would lean my spirit o'er you!
Down the purple of this chamber, tears
    should scarcely run at will.
I am humbled who was humble. Friend,
    —I bow my head before you.
You should lead me to my peasants,—
    but their faces are too still.

There's a lady—an earl's daughter,—
    she is proud and she is noble,
And she treads the crimson carpet, and
    she breathes the perfumed air,
And a kingly blood sends glances up her
    princely eye to trouble,
And the shadow of a monarch's crown
    is softened in her hair.

She has halls among the woodlands,
    she has castles by the breakers,
She has farms and she has manors, she
    can threaten and command,
And the palpitating engines snort in
    steam across her acres,
As they mark upon the blasted heaven
    the measure of the land.

There are none of England's daughters
     who can show a prouder presence;
Upon princely suitors praying, she has
     looked in her disdain.
She was sprung of English nobles,
     I was born of English peasants;
What was *I* that I should love her—
     save for competence to pain?

I was only a poor poet, made for singing
     at her casement,
As the finches or the thrushes, while
     she thought of other things.
Oh, she walked so high above me, she
     appeared to my abasement,
In her lovely silken murmur, like an
     angel clad in wings!

Many vassals bow before her as her
     carriage sweeps their doorways;
She has blest their little children,—as a
     priest or queen were she.
Far too tender, or too cruel far, her
     smile upon the poor was,
For I thought it was the same smile
     which she used to smile on *me*.

She has voters in the Commons, she has
     lovers in the palace;
And of all the fair court-ladies, few have
     jewels half as fine;
Oft the prince has named her beauty
     'twixt the red wine and the chalice.
Oh, and what was *I* to love her? my
     beloved, my Geraldine!

Yet I could not choose but love her.
       I was born to poet-uses,
To love all things set above me, all of
       good and all of fair:
Nymphs of mountain, not of valley, we
       are wont to call the Muses
And in nympholeptic climbing, poets
       pass from mount to star.

And because I was a poet, and because
       the public praised me,
With a critical deduction for the modern
       writer's fault,
I could sit at rich men's tables,—though
       the courtesies that raised me,
Still suggested clear between us the
       pale spectrum of the salt.

And they praised me in her presence;
       —'Will your book appear this summer?'
Then returning to each other—'Yes,
       our plans are for the moors.'
Then with whisper dropped behind me
       —'There he is! the latest comer!
Oh, she only likes his verses! what is
       over, she endures.

'Quite low-born! self-educated! some-
       what gifted though by nature,—
And we make a point of asking him,—
       of being very kind.
You may speak, he does not hear you!
       and besides, he writes no satire,—
All these serpents kept by charmers
       leave the natural sting behind.'

[83]

I grew scornfuller, grew colder, as I
        stood up there among them,
Till as frost intense will burn you, the
        cold scorning scorched my brow;
When a sudden silver speaking, gravely
        cadenced, over-rung them,
And a sudden silken stirring touched
        my inner nature through.

I looked upward and beheld her. With
        a calm and regnant spirit,
Slowly round she swept her eyelids,
        and said clear before them all—
'Have you such superfluous honour, sir,
        that able to confer it
You will come down, Mister Bertram,
        as my guest to Wycombe Hall?'

Here she paused,—she had been paler
        at the first word of her speaking,
But because a silence followed it,
        blushed somewhat, as for shame,
Then, as scorning her own feeling,
        resumed calmly—'I am seeking
More distinction than these gentlemen
        think worthy of my claim.

'Ne'ertheless, you see, I seek it—not
        because I am a woman'
(Here her smile sprang like a fountain,
        and, so, overflowed her mouth),
'But because my woods in Sussex have
        some purple shades at gloaming
Which are worthy of a king in state, or
        poet in his youth.

'I invite you, Mister Bertram, to no
    scene for worldly speeches—
Sir, I scarce should dare—but only where
    God asked the thrushes first—
And if *you* will sing beside them, in the
    covert of my beeches,
I will thank you for the woodlands, . . .
    for the human world, at worst.'

Then she smiled around right childly,
    then she gazed around right queenly,
And I bowed—I could not answer;
    alternated light and gloom—
While as one who quells the lions, with
    a steady eye serenely,
She, with level fronting eyelids, passed
    out stately from the room.

Oh, the blessèd woods of Sussex, I can
    hear them still around me,
With their leafy tide of greenery still
    rippling up the wind.
Oh, the cursèd woods of Sussex! where
    the hunter's arrow found me,
When a fair face and a tender voice had
    made me mad and blind!

In that ancient hall of Wycombe, thronged
    the numerous guests invited,
And the lovely London ladies trod the
    floors with gliding feet;
And their voices low with fashion, not
    with feeling, softly freighted
All the air about the windows, with
    elastic laughters sweet.

For at eve, the open windows flung their
       light out on the terrace,
Which the floating orbs of curtains did
       with gradual shadow sweep,
While the swans upon the river, fed at
       morning by the heiress,
Trembled downward through their
       snowy wings at music in their
       sleep.

And there evermore was music, both of
       instrument and singing,
Till the finches of the shrubberies grew
       restless in the dark;
But the cedars stood up motionless,
       each in a moonlight ringing,
And the deer, half in the glimmer,
       strewed the hollows of the park.

And though sometimes she would bind me
       with her silver-corded speeches
To commix my words and laughter with
       the converse and the jest,
Oft I sate apart, and gazing on the river
       through the beeches,
Heard, as pure the swans swam down
       it, her pure voice o'erfloat the rest.

In the morning, horn of huntsman, hoof
       of steed, and laugh of rider,
Spread out cheery from the court-yard
       till we lost them in the hills,
While herself and other ladies, and her
       suitors left beside her,
Went a-wandering up the gardens
       through the laurels and abeles.

Thus, her foot upon the new-mown grass,
      bareheaded, with the flowing
Of the virginal white vesture gathered
      closely to her throat,—
And the golden ringlets in her neck
      just quickened by her going,
And appearing to breathe sun for air,
      and doubting if to float,—

With a branch of dewy maple, which
      her right hand held above her,
And which trembled a green shadow in
      betwixt her and the skies,
As she turned her face in going, thus,
      she drew me on to love her,
And to worship the divineness of the
      smile hid in her eyes.

For her eyes alone smile constantly:
      her lips have serious sweetness,
And her front is calm—the dimple rarely
      ripples on the cheek;
But her deep blue eyes smile constantly,
      as if they in discreetness
Kept the secret of a happy dream she
      did not care to speak.

Thus she drew me the first morning,
      out across into the garden,
And I walked among her noble friends
      and could not keep behind.
Spake she unto all and unto me—
      'Behold, I am the warden
Of the song-birds in these lindens,
      which are cages to their mind.

'But within this swarded circle, into
        which the lime-walk brings us,
Whence the beeches, rounded greenly,
        stand away in reverent fear,
I will let no music enter, saving what
        the fountain sings us,
Which the lilies round the basin may
        seem pure enough to hear.

'The live air that waves the lilies waves
        the slender jet of water
Like a holy thought sent feebly up from
        soul of fasting saint:
Whereby lies a marble Silence, sleeping!
        (Lough the sculptor wrought her)
So asleep she is forgetting to say Hush!
        —a fancy quaint.

'Mark how heavy white her eyelids!
        not a dream between them lingers,
And the left hand's index droppeth from
        the lips upon the cheek;
While the right hand,—with the symbol
        rose held slack within the fingers,—
Has fallen backward in the basin—yet
        this Silence will not speak!

'That the essential meaning growing
        may exceed the special symbol,
Is the thought as I conceive it: it applies
        more high and low.
Our true noblemen will often through
        right nobleness grow humble,
And assert an inward honour by
        denying outward show.'

'Nay, your Silence,' said I, 'truly, holds
     her symbol rose but slackly,
Yet *she holds it*—or would scarcely be a
     Silence to our ken;
And your nobles wear their ermine on
     the outside, or walk blackly
In the presence of the social law as
     mere ignoble men.

'Let the poets dream such dreaming!
     madam, in these British islands
'Tis the substance that wanes ever, 'tis
     the symbol that exceeds.
Soon we shall have nought but symbol!
     and, for statues like this Silence,
Shall accept the rose's image—in another
     case, the weed's.'

'Not so quickly,' she retorted,—'I confess,
     where'er you go, you
Find for things, names—shows for
     actions, and pure gold for honour clear;
But when all is run to symbol in the
     Social, I will throw you
The world's book which now reads dryly
     and sit down with Silence here.

Half in playfulness she spoke, I thought,
     and half in indignation;
Friends who listened, laughed her words
     off, while her lovers deemed her fair:
A fair woman, flushed with feeling, in
     her noble-lighted station
Near the statue's white reposing—and
     both bathed in sunny air!—

With the trees round, not so distant but
  you heard their vernal murmur,
And beheld in light and shadow the
  leaves in and outward move,
And the little fountain leaping toward
  the sun-heart to be warmer,
Then recoiling in a tremble from the
  too much light above.

'Tis a picture for remembrance. And
  thus, morning after morning,
Did I follow as she drew me by the
  spirit to her feet.
Why, her greyhound followed also!
  dogs—we both were dogs for scorning—
To be sent back when she pleased it and
  her path lay through the wheat.

And thus, morning after morning, spite
  of vows and spite of sorrow,
Did I follow at her drawing, while the
  week-days passed along,
Just to feed the swans this noontide, or
  to see the fawns to-morrow,
Or to teach the hill-side echo some
  sweet Tuscan in a song.

Aye, for sometimes on the hill-side, while
  we sate down in the gowans,
With the forest green behind us, and
  its shadow cast before,
And the river running under, and across
  it from the rowans
A brown partridge whirring near us,
  till we felt the air it bore,—

There, obedient to her praying, did I
    read aloud the poems
Made to Tuscan flutes, or instruments
    more various of our own;
Read the pastoral parts of Spenser—or
    the subtle interflowings
Found in Petrarch's sonnets—here's the
    book—the leaf is folded down!

Or at times a modern volume,—Wordsworth's
    solemn-thoughted idyl,
Howitt's ballad-verse, or Tennyson's
    enchanted reverie,—
Or from Browning some 'Pomegranate,'
    which, if cut deep down the middle,
Shows a heart within blood-tinctured,
    of a veined humanity.

Or at times I read there, hoarsely, some
    new poem of my making:
Poets ever fail in reading their own
    verses to their worth,—
For the echo in you breaks upon the
    words which you are speaking,
And the chariot-wheels jar in the gate
    through which you drive them forth.

After, when we were grown tired of
    books, the silence round us flinging
A slow arm of sweet compression, felt
    with beatings at the breast,
She would break out, on a sudden, in
    a gush of woodland singing,
Like a child's emotion in a god—a naiad
    tired of rest.

Oh, to see or hear her singing! scarce
        I know which is divinest—
For her looks sing too—she modulates
        her gestures on the tune;
And her mouth stirs with the song, like
        song; and when the notes are finest,
'Tis the eyes that shoot out vocal light
        and seem to swell them on.

Then we talked—oh, how we talked! her
        voice, so cadenced in the talking,
Made another singing—of the soul!
        a music without bars;
While the leafy sounds of woodlands,
        humming round where we were walking,
Brought interposition worthy-sweet,—
        as skies about the stars.

And she spake such good thoughts
        natural, as if she always thought them;
She had sympathies so rapid, open, free
        as bird on branch,
Just as ready to fly east as west, which-
        ever way besought them,
In the birchen-wood a chirrup, or a
        cock-crow in the grange.

In her utmost lightness there is truth—
        and often she speaks lightly,
Has a grace in being gay, which even
        mournful souls approve,
For the root of some grave earnest
        thought is understruck so rightly
As to justify the foliage and the waving
        flowers above.

And she talked on—*we* talked, rather!
      upon all things, substance, shadow,
Of the sheep that browsed the grasses,
      of the reapers in the corn,
Of the little children from the schools,
      seen winding through the meadow—
Of the poor rich world beyond them, still
      kept poorer by its scorn.

So, of men, and so, of letters—books are
      men of higher stature,
And the only men that speak aloud for
      future times to hear;
So, of mankind in the abstract, which
      grows slowly into nature,
Yet will lift the cry of 'progress,' as it
      trod from sphere to sphere.

And her custom was to praise me when
      I said,—'The Age culls simples,
With a broad clown's back turned
      broadly to the glory of the stars.
We are gods by our own reck'ning, and
      may well shut up the temples,
And wield on, amid the incense-steam,
      the thunder of our cars.

'For we throw out acclamations of self-
      thanking, self-admiring,
With, at every mile run faster,—"O the
      wondrous wondrous age,"
Little thinking if we work our SOULS as
      nobly as our iron,
Or if angels will commend us at the goal
      of pilgrimage.

'Why, what *is* this patient entrance
     into nature's deep resources,
But the child's most gradual learning to
     walk upright without bane?
When we drive out, from the cloud of
     steam, majestical white horses,
Are we greater than the first men who
     led black ones by the mane?

'If we trod the deeps of ocean, if we
     struck the stars in rising,
If we wrapped the globe intensely with
     one hot electric breath,
'Twere but power within our tether, no
     new spirit-power comprising,
And in life we were not greater men,
     nor bolder men in death.'

She was patient with my talking; and
     I loved her, loved her, certes,
As I loved all heavenly objects, with
     uplifted eyes and hands!
As I loved pure inspirations, loved the
     graces, loved the virtues,
In a Love content with writing his own
     name on desert sands.

Or at least I thought so, purely!—thought
     no idiot Hope was raising
Any crown to crown Love's silence—
     silent Love that sate alone.
Out, alas! the stag is like me—he, that
     tries to go on grazing
With the great deep gun-wound in his
     neck, then reels with sudden moan.

It was thus I reeled. I told you that her
    hand had many suitors;
But she smiles them down imperially,
    as Venus did the waves,
And with such a gracious coldness, that
    they cannot press their futures
On the present of her courtesy, which
    yieldingly enslaves.

And this morning, as I sate alone within
    the inner chamber,
With the great saloon beyond it, lost in
    pleasant thought serene,
For I had been reading Camöens—that
    poem you remember,
Which his lady's eyes are praised in, as
    the sweetest ever seen.

And the book lay open, and my thought
    flew from it, taking from it
A vibration and impulsion to an end
    beyond its own,
As the branch of a green osier, when a
    child would overcome it,
Springs up freely from his clasping and
    goes swinging in the sun.

As I mused I heard a murmur,—it grew
    deep as it grew longer—
Speakers using earnest language—
    'Lady Geraldine, you *would!*'
And I heard a voice that pleaded ever
    on, in accents stronger
As a sense of reason gave it power to
    make its rhetoric good.

Well I knew that voice—it was an earl's,
　　　　of soul that matched his station,
Soul completed into lordship—might and
　　　　right read on his brow;
Very finely courteous—far too proud to
　　　　doubt his domination
Of the common people, he atones for
　　　　grandeur by a bow.

High straight forehead, nose of eagle,
　　　　cold blue eyes, of less expression
Than resistance, coldly casting off the
　　　　looks of other men,
As steel, arrows,—unelastic lips, which
　　　　seem to taste possession,
And be cautious lest the common air
　　　　should injure or distrain.

For the rest, accomplished, upright,—
　　　　aye, and standing by his order
With a bearing not ungraceful; fond of
　　　　art and letters too;
Just a good man made a proud man,—as
　　　　the sandy rocks that border
A wild coast, by circumstances, in a
　　　　regnant ebb and flow.

Thus, I knew that voice—I heard it, and
　　　　I could not help the hearkening.
In the room I stood up blindly, and my
　　　　burning heart within
Seemed to seethe and fuse my senses, till
　　　　they ran on all sides darkening,
And scorched, weighed, like melted metal
　　　　round my feet that stood therein.

And that voice, I heard it pleading, for
      love's sake, for wealth, position,
For the sake of liberal uses, and great
      actions to be done—
And she interrupted gently, 'Nay, my
      lord, the old tradition
Of your Normans, by some worthier hand
      than mine is, should be won.'

'Ah, that white hand!' he said quickly,—
      and in his he either drew it
Or attempted—for with gravity and
      instance she replied,
'Nay, indeed, my lord, this talk is vain,
      and we had best eschew it,
And pass on, like friends, to other points
      less easy to decide.'

What he said again, I know not. It is
      likely that his trouble
Worked his pride up to the surface, for
      she answered in slow scorn,
'And your lordship judges rightly.
      Whom I marry, shall be noble,
Aye, and wealthy. I shall never blush
      to think how he was born.'

There, I maddened! her words stung me.
      Life swept through me into fever,
And my soul sprang up astonished,
      sprang, full-statured in an hour.
Know you what it is when anguish, with
      apocalyptic NEVER,
To a Pythian height dilates you,—and
      despair sublimes to power?

From my brain, the soul-wings budded,—
     waved a flame about my body,
Whence conventions coiled to ashes,
     I felt self-drawn out, as man,
From amalgamate false natures, and I
     saw the skies grow ruddy
With the deepening feet of angels, and
     I knew what spirits can.

I was mad—inspired—say either!
     (anguish worketh inspiration)
Was a man, or beast—perhaps so, for
     the tiger roars, when speared;
And I walked on, step by step, along
     the level of my passion—
Oh my soul! and passed the doorway
     to her face, and never feared.

He had left her, peradventure, when my
     footstep proved my coming—
But for *her*—she half arose, then sate—
     grew scarlet and grew pale.
Oh, she trembled!—'tis so always with
     a worldly man or woman
In the presence of true spirits—what else
     can they do but quail?

Oh, she fluttered like a tame bird, in
     among its forest-brothers
Far too strong for it; then drooping,
     bowed her face upon her hands—
And I spake out wildly, fiercely, brutal
     truths of her and others:
I, she planted in the desert, swathed her,
     windlike, with my sands.

[98]

I plucked up her social fictions, bloody-
      rooted though leaf-verdant,—
Trod them down with words of shaming,
      —all the purple and the gold,
All the 'landed stakes' and lordships,
      all, that spirits pure and ardent
Are cast out of love and honour because
      chancing not to hold.

'For myself I do not argue,' said I,
      'though I love you, madam,
But for better souls that nearer to the
      height of yours have trod;
And this age shows, to my thinking, still
      more infidels to Adam,
Than directly, by profession, simple in-
      fidels to God.

'Yet, O God,' I said, 'O grave,' I said,
      'O mother's heart and bosom,
With whom first and last are equal,
      saint and corpse and little child!
We are fools to your deductions, in these
      figments of heart-closing;
We are traitors to your causes, in these
      sympathies defiled.

'Learn more reverence, madam, not for
      rank or wealth—*that* needs no learning,
That comes quickly—quick as sin does,
      aye, and culminates to sin;
But for Adam's seed, MAN! Trust me,
      'tis a clay above your scorning,
With God's image stamped upon it, and
      God's kindling breath within.

'What right have you, madam, gazing in
      your palace mirror daily,
Getting so by heart your beauty which
      all others must adore,
While you draw the golden ringlets down
      your fingers, to vow gaily
You will wed no man that's only good to
      God, and nothing more?

'Why, what right have you, made fair
      by that same God—the sweetest woman
Of all women He has fashioned—with
      your lovely spirit-face,
Which would seem too near to vanish if
      its smile were not so human,
And your voice of holy sweetness, turning
      common words to grace,

'What right *can* you have, God's other
      works to scorn, despise, revile them
In the gross, as mere men, broadly—not
      as *noble* men, forsooth,—
As mere Parias of the outer world, for-
      bidden to assoil them
In the hope of living, dying, near that
      sweetness of your mouth?

'Have you any answer, madam? If my
      spirit were less earthly,
If its instrument were gifted with a better
      silver string,
I would kneel down where I stand, and
      say—Behold me! I am worthy
Of thy loving, for I love thee! I am
      worthy as a king.

'As it is—your ermined pride, I swear,
        shall feel this stain upon her,
That *I*, poor, weak, tost with passion,
        scorned by me and you again,
Love you, madam—dare to love you—to
        my grief and your dishonour,
To my endless desolation, and your
        impotent disdain!'

More mad words like these—mere madness!
        friend, I need not write them fuller,
For I hear my hot soul dropping on the
        lines in showers of tears.
Oh, a woman! friend, a woman! why,
        a beast had scarce been duller
Than roar bestial loud complaints against
        the shining of the spheres.

But at last there came a pause. I stood
        all vibrating with thunder
Which my soul had used. The silence
        drew her face up like a call.
Could you guess what word she uttered?
        She looked up, as if in wonder,
With tears beaded on her lashes, and
        said 'Bertram!'—it was all.

If she had cursed me, and she might have
        —of if even, with queenly bearing
Which at need is used by women, she
        had risen up and said,
'Sir, you are my guest, and therefore I
        have given you a full hearing,
Now, beseech you, choose a name exact-
        ing somewhat less, instead,'—

[101]

I had borne it!—but that 'Bertram'—
      why it lies there on the paper
A mere word, without her accent,—and
      you cannot judge the weight
Of the calm which crushed my passion:
      I seemed drowning in a vapour,—
And her gentleness destroyed me whom
      her scorn made desolate.

So, struck backward and exhausted by
      that inward flow of passion
Which had rushed on, sparing nothing,
      into forms of abstract truth,
By a logic agonizing through unseemly
      demonstration,
And by youth's own anguish turning
      grimly grey the hairs of youth,—

By the sense accursed and instant, that
      if even I spake wisely
I spake basely—using truth, if what I
      spake, indeed was true,
To avenge wrong on a woman—*her*, who
      sate there weighing nicely
A poor manhood's worth, found guilty of
      such deeds as I could do!—

By such wrong and woe exhausted—
      what I suffered and occasioned,—
As a wild horse through a city runs with
      lightning in his eyes,
And then dashing at a church's cold and
      passive wall, impassioned,
Strikes the death into his burning brain,
      and blindly drops and dies—

So I fell, struck down before her! do
        you blame me, friend, for weakness?
'Twas my strength of passion slew me!
        —fell before her like a stone.
Fast the dreadful world rolled from me,
        on its roaring wheels of blackness—
When the light came, I was lying in this
        chamber, and alone.

Oh, of course, she charged her lacqueys
        to bear out the sickly burden,
And to cast it from her scornful sight—
        but not *beyond* the gate;
She is too kind to be cruel, and too
        haughty not to pardon
Such a man as I—'twere something to
        be level to her hate.

But for me—you now are conscious
        why, my friend, I write this letter,
How my life is read all backward, and
        the charm of life undone:
I shall leave her house at dawn; I would
        to-night, if I were better—
And I charge my soul to hold my body
        strengthened for the sun.

When the sun has dyed the oriel, I depart,
        with no last gazes,
No weak moanings (one word only, left
        in writing for her hands),
Out of reach of all derision, and some
        unavailing praises,
To make front against this anguish in the
        far and foreign lands.

Blame me not. I would not squander
      life in grief—I am abstemious:
I but nurse my spirit's falcon, that its
      wing may soar again.
There's no room for tears of weakness in
      the blind eyes of a Phemius!
Into work the poet kneads them,—and
      he does not die *till then*.

CONCLUSION

Bertram finished the last pages, while
      along the silence ever
Still in hot and heavy splashes, fell the
      tears on every leaf:
Having ended he leans backward in his
      chair, with lips that quiver
From the deep unspoken, aye, and deep
      unwritten thoughts of grief.

Soh! how still the lady standeth! 'tis a
      dream—a dream of mercies!
'Twixt the purple lattice-curtains, how
      she standeth still and pale!
'Tis a vision, sure, of mercies, sent to
      soften his self-curses—
Sent to sweep a patient quiet o'er the
      tossing of his wail.

'Eyes,' he said, 'now throbbing through
      me! are ye eyes that did undo me?
Shining eyes, like antique jewels set in
      Parian statue-stone!
Underneath that calm white forehead, are
      ye ever burning torrid
O'er the desolate sand-desert of my heart
      and life undone?'

With a murmurous stir uncertain, in the
      air, the purple curtain
Swelleth in and swelleth out around her
      motionless pale brows,
While the gliding of the river sends a
      rippling noise for ever
Through the open casement whitened by
      the moonlight's slant repose.

Said he—'Vision of a lady! stand there
      silent, stand there steady!
Now I see it plainly, plainly; now I
      cannot hope or doubt—
There, the brows of mild repression—
      there, the lips of silent passion,
Curvèd like an archer's bow to send the
      bitter arrows out.'

Ever, evermore the while in a slow
      silence she kept smiling,
And approached him slowly, slowly, in
      a gliding measured pace;
With her two white hands extended, as
      if praying one offended,
And a look of supplication, gazing earnest
      in his face.

Said he—'Wake me by no gesture,—
      sound of breath, or stir of vesture!
Let the blessèd apparition melt not yet
      to its divine!
No approaching—hush, no breathing! or
      my heart must swoon to death in
The too utter life thou bringest—O thou
      dream of Geraldine!'

Ever, evermore the while in a slow
      silence she kept smiling—
But the tears ran over lightly from her
      eyes, and tenderly;
'Dost thou, Bertram, truly love me?
      Is no woman far above me
Found more worthy of thy poet-heart
      than such a one as *I?*'

Said he—'I would dream so ever, like
      the flowing of that river,
Flowing ever in a shadow greenly onward
      to the sea!
So, thou vision of all sweetness—princely
      to a full completeness,—
Would my heart and life flow onward—
      deathward—through this dream of THEE!'

Ever, evermore the while in a slow
      silence she kept smiling,
While the silver tears ran faster down
      the blushing of her cheeks;
Then with both her hands enfolding both
      of his, she softly told him,
'Bertram, if I say I love thee, . . . 'tis
      the vision only speaks.'

Softened, quickened to adore her, on his
      knee he fell before her—
And she whispered low in triumph, 'It
      shall be as I have sworn!
Very rich he is in virtues,—very noble—
      noble, certes;
And I shall not blush in knowing that
      men call him lowly born.'

THE LOST BOWER

I

In the pleasant orchard closes,
'God bless all our gains,' say we;
But 'May God bless all our losses,'
Better suits with our degree.
Listen, gentle—ay, and simple! listen, children on the knee!

II

Green the land is where my daily
Steps in jocund childhood played,
Dimpled close with hill and valley,
Dappled very close with shade;
Summer-snow of apple-blossoms running up from glade to
glade.

III

There is one hill I see nearer,
In my vision of the rest;
And a little wood seems clearer
As it climbeth from the west,
Sideway from the tree-locked valley, to the airy upland crest.

IV

Small the wood is, green with hazels,
And, completing the ascent,
Where the wind blows and sun dazzles
Thrills in leafy tremblement,
Like a heart that after climbing beateth quickly through con-
tent.

Not a step the wood advances
O'er the open hill-tops bound;
There, in green arrest, the branches
See their image on the ground:
You may walk beneath them smiling, glad with sight and glad
        with sound.

For you harken on your right hand,
How the birds do leap and call
In the greenwood, out of sight and
Out of reach and fear of all;
And the squirrels crack the filberts through their cheerful
        madrigal.

On your left, the sheep are cropping
The slant grass and daisies pale,
And five apple-trees stand dropping
Separate shadows toward the vale
Over which, in choral silence, the hills look you their 'All hail!'

Far out, kindled by each other,
Shining hills on hills arise,
Close as brother leans to brother
When they press beneath the eyes
Of some father praying blessings from the gifts of paradise.

While beyond, above them mounted,
And above their woods alsò,
Malvern hills, for mountains counted

Not unduly, loom a-row—
Keepers of Piers Plowman's visions through the sunshine and
the snow.

X

Yet, in childhood, little prized I
That fair walk and far survey;
'Twas a straight walk unadvised by
The least mischief worth a nay;
Up and down—as dull as grammar on the eve of holiday.

XI

But the wood, all close and clenching
Bough in bough and root in root,—
No more sky (for over-branching)
At your head than at your foot,—
Oh, the wood drew me within it by a glamour past dispute!

XII

Few and broken paths showed through it,
Where the sheep had tried to run,—
Forced with snowy wool to strew it
Round the thickets, when anon
They, with silly thorn-pricked noses, bleated back into the sun.

XIII

But my childish heart beat stronger
Than those thickets dared to grow:
I could pierce them! *I* could longer
Travel on, methought, than so:
Sheep for sheep-paths! braver children climb and creep where
they would go.

XIV

And the poets wander, (said I,)
Over places all as rude:
Bold Rinaldo's lovely lady
Sate to meet him in a wood:
Rosalinda, like a fountain, laughed out pure with solitude.

XV

And if Chaucer had not travelled
Through a forest by a well,
He had never dreamt nor marvelled
At those ladies fair and fell
Who lived smiling without loving in their island-citadel.

XVI

Thus I thought of the old singers
And took courage from their song,
Till my little struggling fingers
Tore asunder gyve and thong
Of the brambles which entrapped me, and the barrier branches
strong.

XVII

On a day, such pastime keeping,
With a fawn's heart debonair,
Under-crawling, overleaping
Thorns that prick and boughs that bear,
I stood suddenly astonied—I was gladdened unaware.

XVIII

From the place I stood in, floated
Back the covert dim and close,
And the open ground was coated
Carpet-smooth with grass and moss,
And the blue-bell's purple presence signed it worthily across.

XIX

Here a linden-tree stood, bright'ning
All adown its silver rind;
For as some trees draw the lightning,
So this tree, unto my mind,
Drew to earth the blessed sunshine from the sky where it was
      shrined.

XX

Tall the linden-tree and near it
An old hawthorn also grew;
And wood-ivy like a spirit
Hovered dimly round the two,
Shaping thence that bower of beauty which I sing of thus to
      you.

XXI

'Twas a bower for garden fitter
Than for any woodland wide:
Though a fresh and dewy glitter
Struck it through from side to side,
Shaped and shaven was the freshness, as by garden-cunning
      plied.

XXII

Oh, a lady might have come there,
Hooded fairly like her hawk,
With a book or lute in summer,
And a hope of sweeter talk,—
Listening less to her own music than for footsteps on the walk.

XXIII

But that bower appeared a marvel
In the wildness of the place;
With such seeming art and travail,
Finely fixed and fitted was
Leaf to leaf, the dark-green ivy, to the summit from the base.

XXIV

And the ivy veined and glossy
Was enwrought with eglantine;
And the wild hop fibred closely,
And the large-leaved columbine,
Arch of door and window-mullion, did right sylvanly entwine.

XXV

Rose-trees either side the door were
Growing lithe and growing tall,
Each one set, a summer warder
For the keeping of the hall,—
With a red rose and a white rose, leaning, nodding at the wall.

XXVI

As I entered, mosses hushing
Stole all noises from my foot;
And a green elastic cushion,
Clasped within the linden's root,
Took me in a chair of silence very rare and absolute.

XXVII

All the floor was paved with glory,
Greenly, silently inlaid
(Through quick motions made before me)
With fair counterparts in shade
Of the fair serrated ivy-leaves which slanted overhead.

XXVIII

'Is such pavement in a palace?'
So I questioned in my thought:
The sun, shining through the chalice
Of the red rose hung without,
Threw within a red libation, like an answer to my doubt.

XXIX

At the same time, on the linen
Of my childish lap there fell
Two white may-leaves, downward winning
Through the ceiling's miracle,
From a blossom, like an angel, out of sight yet blessing well.

XXX

Down to floor and up to ceiling
Quick I turned my childish face,
With an innocent appealing
For the secret of the place
To the trees, which surely knew it in partaking of the grace.

XXXI

Where's no foot of human creature
How could reach a human hand?
And if this be work of nature,
Why has nature turned so bland,
Breaking off from other wild-work? It was hard to understand.

XXXII

Was she weary of rough-doing,
Of the bramble and the thorn?
Did she pause in tender rueing
Here of all her sylvan scorn?
Or in mock of art's deceiving was the sudden mildness worn?

XXXIII

Or could this same bower (I fancied)
Be the work of Dryad strong,
Who, surviving all that chancéd
In the world's old pagan wrong,
Lay hid, feeding in the woodland on the last true poet's song?

XXXIV

Or was this the house of fairies,
Left, because of the rough ways,
Unassoiled by Ave Marys
Which the passing pilgrim prays,
And beyond St. Catherine's chiming on the blessed Sabbath
days?

XXXV

So, young muser, I sate listening
To my fancy's wildest word.
On a sudden, through the glistening
Leaves around, a little stirred,
Came a sound, a sense of music which was rather felt than
heard.

XXXVI

Softly, finely, it enwound me;
From the world it shut me in,—
Like a fountain falling round me,
Which with silver waters thin
Clips a little water Naiad sitting smilingly within.

XXXVII

Whence the music came, who knoweth?
I know nothing: but indeed
Pan or Faunus never bloweth
So much sweetness from a reed
Which has sucked the milk of waters at the oldest riverhead.

XXXVIII

Never lark the sun can waken
With such sweetness! when the lark,
The high planets overtaking
In the half-evanished Dark,
Casts his singing to their singing, like an arrow to the mark.

Never nightingale so singeth:
Oh, she leans on thorny tree
And her poet-song she flingeth
Over pain to victory!
Yet she never sings such music,—or she sings it not to me.

Never blackbirds, never thrushes
Nor small finches sing so sweet,
When the sun strikes through the bushes
To their crimson clinging feet,
And their pretty eyes look sideways to the summer heavens
complete.

If it _were_ a bird, it seemëd
Most like Chaucer's, which, in sooth,
He of green and azure dreamèd,
While it sate in spirit-ruth
On that bier of a crowned lady, singing nigh her silent mouth.

If it _were_ a bird?—ah, sceptic,
Give me 'yea' or give me 'nay'—
Though my soul were nympholeptic
As I heard that virëlay,
You may stoop your pride to pardon, for my sin is far away!

I rose up in exaltation
And an inward trembling heat,
And (it seemed) in geste of passion
Dropped the music to my feet
Like a garment rustling downwards—such a silence followed
it!

Heart and head beat through the quiet
Full and heavily, though slower:
In the song, I think, and by it,
Mystic Presences of power
Had up-snatched me to the Timeless, then returned me to the
       Hour.

XLV

In a child-abstraction lifted,
Straightway from the bower I past,
Foot and soul being dimly drifted
Through the greenwood, till, at last,
In the hill-top's open sunshine I all consciously was cast.

XLVI

Face to face with the true mountains
I stood silently and still,
Drawing strength from fancy's dauntings,
From the air about the hill
And from Nature's open mercies and most debonair goodwill.

XLVII

Oh, the golden-hearted daisies
Witnessed there, before my youth,
To the truth of things, with praises
Of the beauty of the truth;
And I woke to Nature's real, laughing joyfully for both.

XLVIII

And I said within me, laughing,
'I have found a bower to-day,
A green lusus, fashioned half in
Chance and half in Nature's play;
And a little bird sings nigh it, I will nevermore missay.

'Henceforth, *I* will be the fairy
Of this bower not built by one;
I will go there, sad or merry,
With each morning's benison,
And the bird shall be my harper in the dream-hall I have won.'

So I said. But the next morning,
(—Child, look up into my face—
'Ware, oh sceptic, of your scorning!
This is truth in its pure grace!)
The next morning all had vanished, or my wandering missed
      the place.

Bring an oath most sylvan-holy,
And upon it swear me true—
By the wind-bells swinging slowly
Their mute curfews in the dew,
By the advent of the snow-drop, by the rosemary and rue,—

I affirm by all or any,
Let the cause be charm or chance,
That my wandering searches many
Missed the bower of my romance—
That I nevermore upon it turned my mortal countenance.

I affirm that, since I lost it,
Never bower has seemed so fair;
Never garden-creeper crossed it
With so deft and brave an air,
Never bird sung in the summer, as I saw and heard them there.

LIV

Day by day, with new desire,
Toward my wood I ran in faith,
Under leaf and over brier,
Through the thickets, out of breath;
Like the prince who rescued Beauty from the sleep as long as
  death.

LV

But his sword of mettle clashëd,
And his arm smote strong, I ween,
And her dreaming spirit flashëd
Through her body's fair white screen,
And the light thereof might guide him up the cedar alleys green:

LVI

But for me I saw no splendour—
All my sword was my child-heart;
And the wood refused surrender
Of that bower it held apart,
Safe as Œdipus's grave-place 'mid Colone's olives swart.

LVII

As Aladdin sought the basements
His fair palace rose upon,
And the four-and-twenty casements
Which gave answers to the sun;
So, in wilderment of gazing, I looked up and I looked down.

LVIII

Years have vanished since, as wholly
As the little bower did then;
And you call it tender folly
That such thoughts should come again?
Ah, I cannot change this sighing for your smiling, brother men!

LIX

For this loss it did prefigure
Other loss of better good,
When my soul, in spirit vigour
And in ripened womanhood,
Fell from visions of more beauty than an arbour in a wood.

LX

I have lost—oh, many a pleasure,
Many a hope and many a power—
Studious health and merry leisure,
The first dew on the first flower!
But the first of all my losses was the losing of the bower.

LXI

I have lost the dream of Doing,
And the other dream of Done,
The first spring in the pursuing,
The first pride in the Begun,—
First recoil from incompletion, in the face of what is won—

LXII

Exaltations in the far light
Where some cottage only is;
Mild dejections in the starlight,
Which the sadder-hearted miss;
And the child-cheek blushing scarlet for the very shame of bliss.

LXIII

I have lost the sound child-sleeping
Which the thunder could not break;
Something too of the strong leaping
Of the staglike heart awake,
Which the pale is low for keeping in the road it ought to take.

LXIV

Some respect to social fictions
Has been also lost by me;
And some generous genuflexions,
Which my spirit offered free
To the pleasant old conventions of our false humanity.

LXV

All my losses did I tell you,
Ye perchance would look away,—
Ye would answer me, 'Farewell! you
Make sad company to-day,
And your tears are falling faster than the bitter words you say.'

LXVI

For God placed me like a dial
In the open ground with power,
And my heart had for its trial
All the sun and all the shower:
And I suffered many losses,—and my first was of the bower.

LXVII

Laugh you? If that loss of mine be
Of no heavy-seeming weight—
When the cone falls from the pine-tree,
The young children laugh thereat;
Yet the wind that struck it, riseth, and the tempest shall be
    great.

LXVIII

One who knew me in my childhood
In the glamour and the game,
Looking on me long and mild, would
Never know me for the same.
Come, unchanging recollections, where those changes
        overcame!

LXIX

By this couch I weakly lie on,
While I count my memories,—
Through the fingers which, still sighing,
I press closely on mine eyes,—
Clear as once beneath the sunshine, I behold the bower arise.

LXX

Springs the linden-tree as greenly,
Stroked with light adown its rind;
And the ivy-leaves serenely
Each in either intertwined;
And the rose-trees at the doorway, they have neither grown nor
 pined.

LXXI

From those overblown faint roses
Not a leaf appeareth shed,
And that little bud discloses
Not a thorn's-breadth more of red
For the winters and the summers which have passed me
 overhead.

LXXII

And that music overfloweth,
Sudden sweet, the sylvan eaves:
Thrush or nightingale—who knoweth?
Fay or Faunus—who believes?
But my heart still trembles in me to the trembling of the leaves.

LXXIII

Is the bower lost, then? who sayeth
That the bower indeed is lost?
Hark! my spirit in it prayeth
Through the sunshine and the frost,—
And the prayer preserves it greenly, to the last and uttermost.

[121]

Till another open for me
In God's Eden-land unknown,
With an angel at the doorway,
White with gazing at His throne;
And a saint's voice in the palm-trees, singing—'All is lost . . .
and won!'

RIME OF THE DUCHESS MAY

I

To the belfry, one by one, went the
ringers from the sun,
Toll slowly.
And the oldest ringer said, 'Ours is
music for the Dead,
When the rebecks are all done.'

II

Six abeles i' the churchyard grow on the
northside in a row,
Toll slowly.
And the shadows of their tops rock across
the little slopes
Of the grassy graves below.

III

On the south side and the west, a small
river runs in haste,
Toll slowly.
And between the river flowing and the
fair green trees a-growing
Do the dead lie at their rest.

IV

On the east I sate that day, up against
    a willow grey.
        Toll slowly.
Through the rain of willow-branches, I
    could see the low hill-ranges,
        And the river on its way.

V

There I sate beneath the tree, and the
    bell tolled solemnly,
        Toll slowly.
While the trees' and river's voices flowed
    between the solemn noises,—
        Yet death seemed more loud to me.

VI

There, I read this ancient rime, while
    the bell did all the time
        Toll slowly.
And the solemn knell fell in with the tale
    of life and sin,
        Like a rhythmic fate sublime.

THE RIME

I

Broad the forests stood (I read) on the
    hills of Linteged—
        Toll slowly.
And three hundred years had stood mute
    adown each hoary wood,
        Like a full heart having prayed.

II

And the little birds sang east, and the
    little birds sang west,
      Toll slowly.
And but little thought was theirs of the
    silent antique years,
      In the building of their nest.

III

Down the sun dropt large and red, on
    the towers of Linteged,—
      Toll slowly.
Lance and spear upon the height,
    bristling strange in fiery light,
      While the castle stood in shade.

IV

There, the castle stood up black, with
    the red sun at its back,—
      Toll slowly.
Like a sullen smouldering pyre, with a
    top that flickers fire
      When the wind is on its track.

V

And five hundred archers tall did besiege
    the castle wall,
      Toll slowly.
And the castle, seethed in blood, fourteen
    days and nights had stood,
      And to-night was near its fall.

VI

Yet thereunto, blind to doom, three
    months since, a bride did come,—
      Toll slowly.
One who proudly trod the floors, and
    softly whispered in the doors,
      'May good angels bless our home.'

VII

Oh, a bride of queenly eyes, with a front
    of constancies!
      Toll slowly.
Oh, a bride of cordial mouth,—where the
    untired smile of youth
      Did light outward its own sighs.

VIII

'Twas a Duke's fair orphan-girl, and her
    uncle's ward, the Earl;
      Toll slowly.
Who betrothed her twelve years old, for
    the sake of dowry gold,
      To his son Lord Leigh, the churl.

IX

But what time she had made good all her
    years of womanhood,
      Toll slowly.
Unto both those lords of Leigh, spake
    she out right sovranly,
      'My will runneth as my blood.

X

'And while this same blood makes red
    this same right hand's veins,' she said,—
        Toll slowly.
' 'Tis my will as lady free, not to wed
    a lord of Leigh,
      But Sir Guy of Linteged.'

XI

The old Earl he smilèd smooth, then he
    sighed for wilful youth,—
        Toll slowly.
'Good my niece, that hand withal looketh
    somewhat soft and small
      For so large a will, in sooth.'

XII

She, too, smiled by that same sign,—but
    her smile was cold and fine,—
        Toll slowly.
'Little hand clasps muckle gold, or it
    were not worth the hold
      Of thy son, good uncle mine!'

XIII

Then the young lord jerked his breath,
    and sware thickly in his teeth,
        Toll slowly.
'He would wed his own betrothed, an
    she loved him an she loathed,
      Let the life come or the death.'

XIV

Up she rose with scornful eyes, as her
    father's child might rise,—
      Toll slowly.
'Thy hound's blood, my lord of Leigh,
    stains thy knightly heel,' quoth she,
    'And he moans not where he lies.

XV

'But a woman's will dies hard, in the
    hall or on the sward!'—
      Toll slowly.
'By that grave, my lords, which made me
    orphaned girl and dowered lady,
    I deny you wife and ward.'

XVI

Unto each she bowed her head, and
    swept past with lofty tread.
      Toll slowly.
Ere the midnight-bell had ceased,
    in the chapel had the priest
    Blessed her, bride of Linteged.

XVII

Fast and fain the bridal train along the
    night-storm rode amain.
      Toll slowly.
Hard the steeds of lord and serf struck
    their hoofs out on the turf,
    In the pauses of the rain.

XVIII

Fast and fain the kinsmen's train along
the storm pursued amain—
Toll slowly.
Steed on steed-track, dashing off—
thickening, doubling, hoof on hoof,
In the pauses of the rain.

XIX

And the bridegroom led the flight on his
red-roan steed of might,
Toll slowly.
And the bride lay on his arm, still, as if
she feared no harm,
Smiling out into the night.

XX

'Dost thou fear?' he said at last.—'Nay,'
she answered him in haste,—
Toll slowly.
'Not such death as we could find—only
life with one behind—
Ride on fast as fear—ride fast!'

XXI

Up the mountain wheeled the steed—
girth to ground, and fetlocks
spread,—
Toll slowly.
Headlong bounds, and rocking flanks,—
down he staggered, down the
banks,
To the towers of Linteged.

XXII

High and low the serfs looked out, red
    the flambeaus tossed about,—
       Toll slowly.
In the courtyard rose the cry—'Live the
    Duchess and Sir Guy!'
    But she never heard them shout.

XXIII

On the steed she dropt her cheek, kissed
    his mane and kissed his neck.—
       Toll slowly.
'I had happier died by thee, than lived
    on, a Lady Leigh,'
    Were the first words she did speak.

XXIV

But a three months' joyaunce lay 'twixt
    that moment and to-day,
       Toll slowly.
When five hundred archers tall stand
    beside the castle wall,
    To recapture Duchess May.

XXV

And the castle standeth black, with the
    red sun at its back,—
       Toll slowly.
And a fortnight's siege is done—and,
    except the duchess, none
    Can misdoubt the coming wrack.

XXVI

Then the captain, young Lord Leigh, with
his eyes so grey of blee,
Toll slowly.
And thin lips that scarcely sheath the cold
white gnashing of his teeth,
Gnashed in smiling, absently,

XXVII

Cried aloud, 'So goes the day, bridegroom
fair of Duchess May!'—
Toll slowly.
'Look thy last upon that sun! if thou
seest to-morrow's one,
'Twill be through a foot of clay.

XXVIII

'Ha, fair bride! dost hear no sound, save
that moaning of the hound?'—
Toll slowly.
'Thou and I have parted troth,—yet
I keep my vengeance-oath,
And the other may come round.

XXIX

'Ha! thy will is brave to dare, and thy
new love past compare,'—
Toll slowly.
'Yet thine old love's faulchion brave is
as strong a thing to have
As the will of lady fair.

XXX

'Peck on blindly, netted dove!—If a
    wife's name thee behove,'
      Toll slowly.
'Thou shalt wear the same to morrow,
    ere the grave has hid the sorrow
  Of thy last ill-mated love.

XXXI

'O'er his fixed and silent mouth, thou
    and I will call back troth.'
      Toll slowly.
'He shall altar be and priest,—and he
    will not cry at least
  "I forbid you—I am loath!"'

XXXII

'I will wring thy fingers pale in the
    gauntlet of my mail.'
      Toll slowly.
'"Little hand and muckle gold" close
    shall lie within my hold,
  As the sword did, to prevail.'

XXXIII

Oh, the little birds sang east, and the
    little birds sang west,
      Toll slowly.
Oh, and laughed the Duchess May, and
    her soul did put away
  All his boasting, for a jest.

XXXIV

In her chamber did she sit, laughing low
   to think of it,—
   Toll slowly.
'Tower is strong and will is free—thou
   canst boast, my lord of Leigh,
   But thou boastest little wit.'

XXXV

In her tire-glass gazèd she, and she
   blushed right womanly.
   Toll slowly.
She blushed half from her disdain—half,
   her beauty was so plain,
   —'Oath for oath, my lord of Leigh!'

XXXVI

Straight she called her maidens in—
   'Since ye gave me blame herein,'
   Toll slowly.
'That a bridal such as mine should lack
   gauds to make it fine,
   Come and shrive me from that sin.

XXXVII

'It is three months gone to-day since
   I gave mine hand away.'
   Toll slowly.
'Bring the gold and bring the gem, we
   will keep bride-state in them,
   While we keep the foe at bay.

'On your arms I loose mine hair!—comb
    it smooth and crown it fair.'
    Toll slowly.
'I would look in purple pall from this
    lattice down the wall,
      And throw scorn to one that's
      there!'

Oh, the little birds sang east, and the
    little birds sang west.
    Toll slowly.
On the tower the castle's lord leant in
    silence on his sword,
      With an anguish in his breast.

With a spirit-laden weight, did he lean
    down passionate.
    Toll slowly.
They have almost sapped the wall,—they
    will enter therewithal,
      With no knocking at the gate.

Then the sword he leant upon, shivered,
    snapped upon the stone,—
    Toll slowly.
'Sword,' he thought, with inward laugh,
    'ill thou servest for a staff
      When thy nobler use is done!

XLII

'Sword, thy nobler use is done!—tower
is lost, and shame begun!'—
Toll slowly.
'If we met them in the breach, hilt to
hilt or speech to speech,
We should die there, each for one.

XLIII

'If we met them at the wall, we should
singly, vainly fall,'—
Toll slowly.
'But if *I* die here alone,—then I die,
who am but one,
And die nobly for them all.

XLIV

'Five true friends lie for my sake, in the
moat and in the brake,'—
Toll slowly.
'Thirteen warriors lie at rest, with a
black wound in the breast,
And not one of these will wake.

XLV

'So no more of this shall be!—heart-blood
weighs too heavily,'—
Toll slowly.
'And I could not sleep in grave, with the
faithful and the brave
Heaped around and over me.

XLVI

'Since young Clare a mother hath, and
    young Ralph a plighted faith,'—
      Toll slowly.
'Since my pale young sister's cheeks
    blush like rose when Ronald speaks,
Albeit never a word she saith—

XLVII

'These shall never die for me—life-blood
    falls too heavily:'
      Toll slowly.
'And if *I* die here apart,—o'er my dead
    and silent heart
They shall pass out safe and free.

XLVIII

'When the foe hath heard it said—
    "Death holds Guy of Linteged,"'
      Toll slowly.
'That new corse new peace shall bring,
    and a blessèd, blessèd thing
Shall the stone be at its head.

XLIX

'Then my friends shall pass out free, and
    shall bear my memory,'—
      Toll slowly.
'Then my foes shall sleek their pride,
    soothing fair my widowed bride,
Whose sole sin was love of me.

'With their words all smooth and sweet,
    they will front her and entreat,'
      Toll slowly.
'And their purple pall will spread under-
    neath her fainting head
    While her tears drop over it.

'She will weep her woman's tears, she
    will pray her woman's prayers,'—
      Toll slowly.
'But her heart is young in pain, and her
    hopes will spring again
    By the suntime of her years.

'Ah, sweet May! ah, sweetest grief!—
    once I vowed thee my belief,'
      Toll slowly.
'That thy name expressed thy sweetness,
    —May of poets, in completeness!
    Now my May-day seemeth brief.'

All these silent thoughts did swim o'er
    his eyes grown strange and dim,—
      Toll slowly.
Till his true men in the place, wished
    they stood there face to face
    With the foe instead of him.

LIV

'One last oath, my friends that wear
    faithful hearts to do and dare!'—
      Toll slowly.
'Tower must fall, and bride be lost!—
    swear me service worth the cost!'
    —Bold they stood around to swear.

LV

'Each man clasp my hand and swear, by
    the deed we failed in there,'
      Toll slowly.
'Not for vengeance, not for right, will
    ye strike one blow to-night!'
    —Pale they stood around to swear.

LVI

'One last boon, young Ralph and Clare!
    faithful hearts to do and dare!'—
      Toll slowly.
'Bring that steed up from his stall, which
    she kissed before you all!
    Guide him up the turret-stair.

LVII

'Ye shall harness him aright, and lead
    upward to this height.'
      Toll slowly.
'Once in love and twice in war hath he
    borne me strong and far:
    He shall bear me far to-night.'

Then his men looked to and fro, when
    they heard him speaking so.
      Toll slowly.
—"Las! the noble heart,' they thought,—
    'he in sooth is grief-distraught:
    Would we stood here with the foe!'

But a fire flashed from his eye, 'twixt
    their thought and their reply,—
      Toll slowly.
'Have ye so much time to waste? We
    who ride here, must ride fast,
    As we wish our foes to fly.'

They have fetched the steed with care,
    in the harness he did wear,
      Toll slowly.
Past the court, and through the doors,
    across the rushes of the floors,
    But they goad him up the stair.

Then from out her bower chambère, did
    the Duchess May repair.
      Toll slowly.
'Tell me now what is your need,' said
    the lady, 'of this steed,
    That ye goad him up the stair?'

Calm she stood; unbodkined through, fell
    her dark hair to her shoe,—
      Toll slowly.
And the smile upon her face, ere she
    left the tiring-glass,
      Had not time enough to go.

'Get thee back, sweet Duchess May!
    hope is gone like yesterday,'—
      Toll slowly.
'One half-hour completes the breach;
    and thy lord grows wild of speech!
      Get thee in, sweet lady, and pray.

'In the east tower, high'st of all, loud
    he cries for steed from stall.'
      Toll slowly.
'He would ride as far,' quoth he, 'as
    for love and victory,
      Though he rides the castle-wall.'

'And we fetch the steed from stall, up
    where never a hoof did fall.'—
      Toll slowly.
'Wifely prayer meets deathly need!
    may the sweet Heavens hear thee plead
      If he rides the castle-wall.'

LXVI

Low she dropt her head, and lower, till
    her hair coiled on the floor,—
      Toll slowly.
And tear after tear you heard fall dis-
    tinct as any word
      Which you might be listening for.

LXVII

'Get thee in, thou soft ladye!—here is
    never a place for thee!'—
      Toll slowly.
'Braid thine hair and clasp thy gown,
    that thy beauty in its moan
      May find grace with Leigh of Leigh.'

LXVIII

She stood up in bitter case, with a pale
    yet steady face,
      Toll slowly.
Like a statue thunderstruck, which,
    though quivering, seems to look
      Right against the thunder-place.

LXIX

And her foot trod in, with pride, her
    own tears i' the stone beside.—
      Toll slowly.
'Go to, faithful friends, go to!—judge
    no more what ladies do,—
      No, nor how their lords may ride!'

LXX

Then the good steed's rein she took, and
    his neck did kiss and stroke:
      Toll slowly.
Soft he neighed to answer her, and then
    followed up the stair,
      For the love of her sweet look.

LXXI

Oh, and steeply, steeply wound up the
    narrow stair around!
      Toll slowly.
Oh, and closely, closely speeding, step
    by step beside her treading,
      Did he follow, meek as hound.

LXXII

On the east tower, high'st of all,—there,
    where never a hoof did fall,—
      Toll slowly.
Out they swept, a vision steady,—noble
    steed and lovely lady,
      Calm as if in bower or stall.

LXXIII

Down she knelt at her lord's knee, and
    she looked up silently,—
      Toll slowly.
And he kissed her twice and thrice, for
    that look within her eyes
      Which he could not bear to see.

LXXIV

Quoth he, 'Get thee from this strife,—
    and the sweet saints bless thy life!'—
      Toll slowly.
'In this hour, I stand in need of my
    noble red-roan steed,
      But no more of my noble wife.'

LXXV

Quoth she, 'Meekly have I done all thy
    biddings under sun;'
      Toll slowly.
'But by all my womanhood, which is
    proved so, true and good,
      I will never do this one.

LXXVI

'Now by womanhood's degree, and by
    wifehood's verity,'
      Toll slowly.
'In this hour if thou hast need of thy
    noble red-roan steed,
      Thou hast also need of *me*.

LXXVII

'By this golden ring ye see on this
    lifted hand, pardiè,'
      Toll slowly.
'If, this hour, on castle-wall, can be
    room for steed from stall,
      Shall be also room for *me*.

LXXVIII

'So the sweet saints with me be' (did
    she utter solemnly)
       Toll slowly.
'If a man, this eventide, on this castle
    wall will ride,
      He shall ride the same with *me*.'

LXXIX

Oh, he sprang up in the selle, and he
    laughed out bitter-well,—
       Toll slowly.
'Wouldst thou ride among the leaves,
    as we used on other eves,
      To hear chime a vesper-bell?'

LXXX

She clang closer to his knee—'Aye, be-
    neath the cypress-tree!'—
       Toll slowly.
'Mock me not, for otherwhere than along
    the greenwood fair
      Have I ridden fast with thee.

LXXXI

'Fast I rode with new-made vows, from
    my angry kinsman's house.'
       Toll slowly.
'What, and would you men should reck
    that I dared more for love's sake
      As a bride than as a spouse?

LXXXII

'What, and would you it should fall, as
    a proverb, before all,'
     Toll slowly.
'That a bride may keep your side while
    through castle-gate you ride,
     Yet eschew the castle-wall?'

LXXXIII

Ho! the breach yawns into ruin, and
    roars up against her suing,
     Toll slowly.
With the inarticulate din, and the
    dreadful falling in—
     Shrieks of doing and undoing!

LXXXIV

Twice he wrung her hands in twain,
    but the small hands closed again.
     Toll slowly.
Back he reined the steed—back, back!
    but she trailed along his track
     With a frantic clasp and strain.

LXXXV

Evermore the foemen pour through the
    crash of window and door,—
     Toll slowly.
And the shouts of Leigh and Leigh, and
    the shrieks of 'kill!' and 'flee!'
     Strike up clear amid the roar.

LXXXVI

Thrice he wrung her hands in twain,—
    but they closed and clung again,—
    Toll slowly.
Wild she clung, as one, withstood,
    clasps a Christ upon the rood,
In a spasm of deathly pain.

LXXXVII

She clung wild and she clung mute,
    with her shuddering lips half-shut.
    Toll slowly.
Her head fallen as half in swound,—
    hair and knee swept on the ground,
She clung wild to stirrup and foot.

LXXXVIII

Back he reined his steed back-thrown
    on the slippery coping-stone:
    Toll slowly.
Back the iron hoofs did grind on the
    battlement behind
Whence a hundred feet went down.

LXXXIX

And his heel did press and goad on the
    quivering flank bestrode,—
    Toll slowly.
'Friends and brothers, save my wife!—
    Pardon, sweet, in change for life,—
But I ride alone to God.'

XC

Straight as if the Holy name had up-
    breathed her like a flame,
      Toll slowly.
She upsprang, she rose upright,—in his
    selle she sate in sight,
      By her love she overcame.

XCI

And her head was on his breast, where
    she smiled as one at rest,—
      Toll slowly.
'Ring,' she cried, 'O vesper-bell, in the
    beechwood's old chapelle!
      But the passing-bell rings best.'

XCII

They have caught out at the rein, which
    Sir Guy threw loose—in vain,—
      Toll slowly.
For the horse in stark despair, with his
    front hoofs poised in air,
      On the last verge rears amain.

XCIII

Now he hangs, he rocks between, and
    his nostrils curdle in!—
      Toll slowly.
Now he shivers head and hoof—and the
    flakes of foam fall off,
      And his face grows fierce and thin!

And a look of human woe from his
  staring eyes did go,
   Toll slowly.
And a sharp cry uttered he, in a foretold
  agony
  Of the headlong death below,—

And, 'Ring, ring, thou passing-bell,'
  still she cried, 'i' the old chapelle!'—
   Toll slowly.
Then back-toppling, crashing back—
  a dead weight flung out to wrack,
  Horse and riders overfell.

* * *

Oh, the little birds sang east, and the
  little birds sang west,
   Toll slowly.
And I read this ancient Rime, in the
  churchyard, while the chime
  Slowly tolled for one at rest.

The abeles moved in the sun, and the
  river smooth did run,
   Toll slowly.
And the ancient Rime rang strange,
  with its passion and its change,
  Here, where all done lay undone.

III

And beneath a willow tree, I a little
    grave did see,
      Toll slowly.
Where was graved,—HERE UNDEFILED,
    LIETH MAUD, A THREE-YEAR CHILD,
    EIGHTEEN HUNDRED, FORTY-THREE.

IV

Then, O spirits, did I say, ye who rode
    so fast that day,—
      Toll slowly.
Did star-wheels and angel wings, with
    their holy winnowings,
    Keep beside you all the way?

V

Though in passion ye would dash, with
    a blind and heavy crash,
      Toll slowly.
Up against the thick-bossed shield of
    God's judgement in the field,—
    Though your heart and brain were rash,—

VI

Now, your will is all unwilled—now,
    your pulses are all stilled!
      Toll slowly.
Now, ye lie as meek and mild (whereso
    laid) as Maud the child,
    Whose small grave was lately filled.

VII

Beating heart and burning brow, ye are
    very patient now,
       Toll slowly.
And the children might be bold to pluck
    the kingcups from your mould
     Ere a month had let them grow.

VIII

And you let the goldfinch sing in the alder
    near in spring,
       Toll slowly.
Let her build her nest and sit all the
    three weeks out on it,
     Murmuring not at anything.

IX

In your patience ye are strong; cold
    and heat ye take not wrong.
       Toll slowly.
When the trumpet of the angel blows
    eternity's evangel,
     Time will seem to you not long.

X

Oh, the little birds sang east, and the
    little birds sang west,
       Toll slowly.
And I said in underbreath,—All our life
    is mixed with death,
     And who knoweth which is best?

Oh, the little birds sang east, and the
little birds sang west,
Toll slowly.
And I smiled to think God's greatness
flowed around our incompleteness,—
Round our restlessness, His rest.

THE LADY'S YES

I

'Yes,' I answered you last night;
'No,' this morning, sir, I say.
Colours seen by candle-light
Will not look the same by day.

II

When the viols played their best,
Lamps above and laughs below,
Love me sounded like a jest,
Fit for *yes* or fit for *no*.

III

Call me false or call me free—
Vow, whatever light may shine,
No man on your face shall see
Any grief for change on mine.

IV

Yet the sin is on us both;
Time to dance is not to woo;
Wooing light makes fickle troth,
Scorn of *me* recoils on *you*.

Learn to win a lady's faith
  Nobly as the thing is high,
Bravely, as for life and death—
  With a loyal gravity.

Lead her from the festive boards,
  Point her to the starry skies;
Guard her, by your truthful words,
  Pure from courtship's flatteries.

By your truth she shall be true,
  Ever true, as wives of yore;
And her *yes*, once said to you,
  SHALL be Yes for evermore.

BERTHA IN THE LANE

I

Put the broidery-frame away,
  For my sewing is all done:
The last thread is used to-day,
  And I need not join it on.
Though the clock stands at the noon
I am weary. I have sewn,
Sweet, for thee, a wedding gown.

Sister, help me to the bed,
    And stand near me, Dearest-sweet.
Do not shrink nor be afraid,
    Blushing with a sudden heat!
No one standeth in the street?—
By God's love I go to meet,
Love I thee with love complete.

Lean thy face down; drop it in
    These two hands, that I may hold
Twixt their palms thy cheek and chin,
    Stroking back the curls of gold:
Tis a fair, fair face, in sooth—
Larger eyes and redder mouth
Than mine were in my first youth.

Thou art younger by seven years—
    Ah!—so bashful at my gaze,
That the lashes, hung with tears,
    Grow too heavy to upraise?
I would wound thee by no touch
Which thy shyness feels as such:
Dost though mind me, Dear, so much?

Have I not been nigh a mother
    To thy sweetness—tell me, Dear?
Have we not loved one another
    Tenderly, from year to year,
Since our dying mother mild
Said with accents undefiled,
'Child, be mother to this child!'

VI

Mother, mother, up in heaven,
   Stand up on the jasper sea,
And be witness I have given
   All the gifts required of me,—
Hope that blessed me, bliss that crowned.
Love that left me with a wound,
Life itself that turneth round!

VII

Mother, mother, thou art kind,
   Thou art standing in the room,
In a molten glory shrined
   That rays off into the gloom!
But thy smile is bright and bleak
Like cold waves—I cannot speak,
I sob in it, and grow weak.

VIII

Ghostly mother, keep aloof
   One hour longer from my soul,
For I still am thinking of
   Earth's warm-beating joy and dole!
On my finger is a ring
Which I still see glittering
When the night hides everything.

IX

Little sister, thou art pale!
   Ah, I have a wandering brain—
But I lose that fever-bale,
   And my thoughts grow calm again.
Lean down closer—closer still!
I have words thine ear to fill,—
And would kiss thee at my will.

X

Dear, I heard thee in the spring,
　　Thee and Robert—through the trees,—
When we all went gathering
　　Boughs of May-bloom for the bees.
Do not start so! think instead
How the sunshine overhead
Seemed to trickle through the shade.

XI

What a day it was, that day!
　　Hills and vales did openly
Seem to heave and throb away
　　At the sight of the great sky;
And the silence, as it stood
In the glory's golden flood,
Audibly did bud, and bud.

XII

Through the winding hedgerows green,
　　How we wandered, I and you,—
With the bowery tops shut in,
　　And the gates that showed the view!
How we talked there! thrushes soft
Sang our praises out, or oft
Bleatings took them, from the croft:

XIII

Till the pleasure grown too strong
　　Left me muter evermore,
And, the winding road being long,
　　I walked out of sight, before,
And so, wrapt in musings fond,
Issued (past the wayside pond)
On the meadow-lands beyond.

XIV

I sate down beneath the beech
  Which leans over to the lane,
And the far sound of your speech
  Did not promise any pain;
And I blessed you full and free,
With a smile stooped tenderly
O'er the May-flowers on my knee.

XV

But the sound grew into word
  As the speakers drew more near—
Sweet, forgive me that I heard
  What you wished me not to hear.
Do not weep so—do not shake—
Oh,—I heard thee, Bertha, make
Good true answers for my sake.

XVI

Yes, and HE too! let him stand
  In thy thoughts untouched by blame.
Could he help it, if my hand
  He had claimed with hasty claim?
That was wrong perhaps—but then
Such things be—and will, again.
Women cannot judge for men.

XVII

Had he seen thee when he swore
  He would love but me alone?
Thou wast absent, sent before
  To our kin in Sidmouth town.
When we saw thee who art best
Past compare, and loveliest,
He but judged thee as the rest.

XVIII

Could we blame him with grave words,
 Thou and I, Dear, if we might?
Thy brown eyes have looks like birds
 Flying straightway to the light:
Mine are older.—Hush!—look out—
Up the street! Is none without?
How the poplar swings about!

XVIX

And that hour—beneath the beech,
 When I listened in a dream,
And he said in his deep speech
 That he owed me all *esteem*,—
Each word swam in on my brain
With a dim, dilating pain,
Till it burst with that last strain.

XX

I fell flooded with a dark,
 In the silence of a swoon.
When I rose, still cold and stark,
 There was night,—I saw the moon:
And the stars, each in its place,
And the May-blooms on the grass,
Seemed to wonder what I was.

XXI

And I walked as if apart
 From myself, when I could stand—
And I pitied my own heart,
 As if I held it in my hand,
Somewhat coldly,—with a sense
Of fulfilled benevolence,
And a 'Poor thing' negligence.

XXII

And I answered coldly too,
    When you met me at the door;
And I only *heard* the dew
    Dripping from me to the floor;
And the flowers I bade you see,
Were too withered for the bee,—
As my life, henceforth, for me.

XXIII

Do not weep so—Dear—heart-warm!
    All was best as it befell.
If I say he did me harm,
    I speak wild,—I am not well.
All his words were kind and good—
He esteemed me. Only, blood
Runs so faint in womanhood!

XXIV

Then I always was too grave,—
    Liked the saddest ballad sung,—
With that look, besides, we have
    In our faces, who die young.
I had died, Dear, all the same;
Life's long, joyous, jostling game
Is too loud for my meek shame.

XXV

We are so unlike each other,
    Thou and I, that none could guess
We were children of one mother,
    But for mutual tenderness.
Thou art rose-lined from the cold,
And meant verily to hold
Life's pure pleasures manifold.

XXVI

I am pale as crocus grows
    Close behind a rose-tree's root;
Whosoe'er would reach the rose,
    Treads the crocus underfoot.
I, like May-bloom on thorn-tree,
Thou, like merry summer-bee!
Fit that I be plucked for thee!

XXVII

Yet who plucks me?—no one mourns,
    I have lived my season out,
And now die of my own thorns
    Which I could not live without.
Sweet, be merry! How the light
Comes and goes! If it be night,
Keep the candles in my sight.

XXVIII

Are there footsteps at the door?
    Look out quickly. Yea, or nay?
Some one might be waiting for
    Some last word that I might say.
Nay? So best!—so angels would
Stand off clear from deathly road,
Not to cross the sight of God.

XXIX

Colder grow my hands and feet.
    When I wear the shroud I made,
Let the folds lie straight and neat,
    And the rosemary be spread,
That if any friend should come,
(To see *thee*, Sweet!) all the room
May be lifted out of gloom.

And, dear Bertha, let me keep
   On my hand this little ring,
Which at nights, when others sleep,
   I can still see glittering.
Let me wear it out of sight,
In the grave,—where it will light
All the dark up, day and night.

On that grave drop not a tear!
   Else, though fathom-deep the place,
Through the woollen shroud I wear
   I shall feel it on my face.
Rather smile there, blessëd one,
Thinking of me in the sun,
Or forget me—smiling on!

Art thou near me? nearer? so!
   Kiss me close upon the eyes,
That the earthly light may go
   Sweetly, as it used to rise,
When I watched the morning-grey
Strike, betwixt the hills, the way
He was sure to come that day.

So,—no more vain words be said!
   The hosannas nearer roll.
Mother, smile now on thy Dead,
   I am death-strong in my soul.
Mystic Dove alit on cross,
Guide the poor bird of the snows
Through the snow-wind above loss!

XXXIV

Jesus, Victim, comprehending
   Love's divine self-abnegation,
Cleanse my love in its self-spending,
   And absorb the poor libation!
Wind my thread of life up higher.
Up, through angels' hands of fire!
I aspire while I expire.

LOVED ONCE

I

I classed, appraising once,
Earth's lamentable sounds,—the welladay,
   The jarring yea and nay,
The fall of kisses on unanswering clay,
The sobbed farewell, the welcome mournfuller,—
   But all did leaven the air
With a less bitter leaven of sure despair
   Than these words—'I loved ONCE.'

II

And who saith 'I loved ONCE'?
Not angels,—whose clear eyes, love, love foresee,
   Love, through eternity,
And by To Love do apprehend To Be.
Not God, called LOVE, His noble crown-name, casting
   A light too broad for blasting!
The great God changing not from everlasting,
   Saith never 'I loved ONCE.'

III

Oh, never is 'Loved ONCE'
Thy word, thou Victim-Christ, misprizèd friend!
    Thy cross and curse may rend,
But having loved Thou lovest to the end.
This is man's saying—man's. Too weak to move
    One spherèd star above,
Man desecrates the eternal God-word Love
    By his No More, and Once.

IV

How say ye 'We loved once,'
Blasphemers? Is your earth not cold enow,
    Mourners, without that snow?
Ah, friends! and would ye wrong each other so?
And could ye say of some whose love is known,
    Whose prayers have met your own,
Whose tears have fallen for you, whose smiles have shone
    So long,—'We loved them ONCE'?

V

Could ye 'We loved her once'
Say calm of me, sweet friends, when out of sight?
    When hearts of better right
Stand in between me and your happy light?
Or when, as flowers kept too long in the shade,
    Ye find my colours fade,
And all that is not love in me, decayed?
    Such words—Ye loved me ONCE!

VI

Could ye 'We loved her once'
Say cold of me when further put away
   In earth's sepulchral clay,—
When mute the lips which deprecate to-day?
Not so! not then—least then. When life is shriven,
   And death's full joy is given,—
Of those who sit and love you up in heaven,
   Say not 'We loved them once.'

VII

Say never, ye loved ONCE.
God is too near above, the grave, beneath,
   And all our moments breathe
Too quick in mysteries of life and death,
For such a word. The eternities avenge
   Affections light of range.
There comes no change to justify that change,
   Whatever comes—Loved ONCE!

VIII

And yet that same word ONCE
Is humanly acceptive. Kings have said,
   Shaking a discrowned head,
'We ruled once,'—dotards, 'We once taught and led.'
Cripples once danced i' the vines—and bards approved
   Were once by scornings moved:
But love strikes one hour—LOVE! those *never* loved
   Who dream that they loved ONCE.

CATARINA TO CAMOENS

I

On the door you will not enter,
   I have gazed too long—adieu!
Hope withdraws her peradventure—
   Death is near me,—and not *you*.
     Come, O lover,
     Close and cover
These poor eyes, you called, I ween,
'Sweetest eyes, were ever seen.'

II

When I heard you sing that burden
   In my vernal days and bowers,
Other praises disregarding,
   I but hearkened that of yours—
     Only saying
     In heart-playing,
'Blessed eyes mine eyes have been,
If the sweetest, HIS have seen!'

III

But all changes. At this vesper,
   Cold the sun shines down the door.
If you stood there, would you whisper
   'Love, I love you,' as before,—
     Death pervading
     Now, and shading
Eyes you sang of, that yestreen,
As the sweetest ever seen?

[163]

IV

Yes, I think, were you beside them,
  Near the bed I die upon,—
Though their beauty you denied them,
  As you stood there, looking down,
      You would truly
      Call them duly,
For the love's sake found therein,—
'Sweetest eyes, were ever seen.'

V

And if *you* looked down upon them,
  And if *they* looked up to *you*,
All the light which has foregone them
  Would be gathered back anew.
      They would truly
      Be as duly
Love-transformed to beauty's sheen,—
'Sweetest eyes, were ever seen.'

VI

But, ah me! you only see me,
  In your thoughts of loving man,
Smiling soft perhaps and dreamy
  Through the wavings of my fan,—
      And unweeting
      Go repeating,
In your reverie serene,
'Sweetest eyes, were ever seen.'

While my spirit leans and reaches
　From my body still and pale,
Fain to hear what tender speech is
　In your love to help my bale—
　　　O my poet,
　　　Come and show it!
Come, of latest love, to glean
'Sweetest eyes, were ever seen.'

O my poet, O my prophet,
　When you praised their sweetness so,
Did you think, in singing of it,
　That it might be near to go?
　　　Had you fancies
　　　From their glances,
That the grave would quickly screen
'Sweetest eyes, were ever seen'?

No reply! the fountain's warble
　In the court-yard sounds alone.
As the water to the marble
　So my heart falls with a moan
　　　From love-sighing
　　　To this dying.
Death forerunneth Love to win
'Sweetest eyes, were ever seen.'

X

Will you come? When I'm departed
    Where all sweetnesses are hid;
Where thy voice, my tender-hearted,
    Will not lift up either lid.
        Cry, O lover,
        Love is over!
Cry beneath the cypress green—
'Sweetest eyes, were ever seen.'

XI

When the angelus is ringing,
    Near the convent will you walk,
And recall the choral singing
    Which brought angels down our talk?
        Spirit-shriven
        I viewed Heaven,
Till you smiled—'Is earth unclean,
Sweetest eyes, were ever seen?'

XII

When beneath the palace-lattice,
    You ride slow as you have done,
And you see a face there—that is
    Not the old familiar one,—
        Will you oftly
        Murmur softly,
'Here, ye watched me morn and e'en,
Sweetest eyes, were ever seen'?

XIII

When the palace-ladies, sitting
   Round your gittern, shall have said,
'Poet, sing those verses written
   For the lady who is dead,'
      Will you tremble,
      Yet dissemble,—
Or sing hoarse, with tears between,
'Sweetest eyes, were ever seen'?

XIV

'Sweetest eyes!' how sweet in flowings
   The repeated cadence is!
Though you sang a hundred poems,
   Still the best one would be this.
      I can hear it
      'Twixt my spirit
And the earth-noise intervene—
'Sweetest eyes, were ever seen!'

XV

But the priest waits for the praying,
   And the choir are on their knees,
And the soul must pass away in
   Strains more solemn high than these.
      Miserere
      For the weary!
Oh, no longer for Catrine,
'Sweetest eyes, were ever seen!'

XVI

Keep my ribbon, take and keep it
  (I have loosed it from my hair),
Feeling, while you overweep it,
  Not alone in your despair,
    Since with saintly
    Watch unfaintly
Out of heaven shall o'er you lean
'Sweetest eyes, were ever seen.'

XVII

But—but *now*—yet unremovèd
  Up to Heaven, they glisten fast.
You may cast away, Belovèd,
  In your future all my past.
    Such old phrases
    May be praises
For some fairer bosom-queen—
'Sweetest eyes, were ever seen!'

XVIII

Eyes of mine, what are ye doing?
  Faithless, faithless,—praised amiss
If a tear be of your showing,
  Dropt for any hope of HIS!
    Death has boldness
    Besides coldness,
If unworthy tears demean
'Sweetest eyes, were ever seen.'

XIX

I will look out to his future;
　I will bless it till it shine.
Should he ever be a suitor
　Unto sweeter eyes than mine,
　　Sunshine gild them,
　　Angels shield them,
Whatsoever eyes terrene
Be the sweetest HIS have seen!

THE ROMANCE OF THE SWAN'S NEST

I

Little Ellie sits alone
'Mid the beeches of a meadow
　By a stream-side on the grass,
　And the trees are showering down
Doubles of their leaves in shadow
　On her shining hair and face.

II

She has thrown her bonnet by,
And her feet she has been dipping
　In the shallow water's flow;
　Now she holds them nakedly
In her hands, all sleek and dripping,
　While she rocketh to and fro.

III

Little Ellie sits alone,
And the smile she softly uses
    Fills the silence like a speech,
    While she thinks what shall be done,—
And the sweetest pleasure chooses
    For her future within reach.

IV

Little Ellie in her smile
Chooses—'I will have a lover,
    Riding on a steed of steeds!
    He shall love me without guile,
And to *him* I will discover
    The swan's nest among the reeds.

V

'And the steed shall be red-roan,
And the lover shall be noble,
    With an eye that takes the breath;
    And the lute he plays upon
Shall strike ladies into trouble,
    As his sword strikes men to death.

VI

'And the steed it shall be shod
All in silver, housed in azure,
    And the mane shall swim the wind;
    And the hoofs along the sod
Shall flash onward and keep measure,
    Till the shepherds look behind.

'But my lover will not prize
All the glory that he rides in,
   When he gazes in my face:
   He will say, 'O Love, thine eyes
Build the shrine my soul abides in,
   And I kneel here for thy grace!'

'Then, aye, then he shall kneel low,
With the red-roan steed anear him
   Which shall seem to understand,—
   Till I answer, 'Rise and go!
For the world must love and fear him
   Whom I gift with heart and hand.'

'Then he will arise so pale,
I shall feel my own lips tremble
   With a *yes* I must not say,
   Nathless maiden-brave, 'Farewell,'
I will utter, and dissemble—
   'Light to-morrow with to-day!'

'Then he'll ride among the hills
To the wide world past the river,
   There to put away all wrong;
   To make straight distorted wills,
And to empty the broad quiver
   Which the wicked bear along.

'Three times shall a young foot-page
Swim the stream and climb the mountain
   And kneel down beside my feet—
   'Lo, my master sends this gage,
Lady, for thy pity's counting!
   What wilt thou exchange for it?'

   'And the first time, I will send
A white rosebud for a guerdon,
   And the second time, a glove;
   But the third time—I may bend
From my pride, and answer—'Pardon,
   If he comes to take my love.'

   'Then the young foot-page will run,
Then my lover will ride faster,
   Till he kneeleth at my knee:
   'I am a duke's eldest son!
Thousand serfs do call me master,—
   But, O Love, I love but *thee*!'

   'He will kiss me on the mouth
Then, and lead me as a lover
   Through the crowds that praise his deeds:
   And, when soul-tied by one troth,
Unto *him* I will discover
   That swan's nest among the reeds.'

XV

Little Ellie, with her smile
Not yet ended, rose up gaily,
  Tied the bonnet, donned the shoe,
  And went homeward round a mile,
Just to see, as she did daily,
  What more eggs were with the two.

XVI

Pushing through the elm-tree copse,
Winding up the stream, light-hearted,
  Where the osier pathway leads—
Past the boughs she stoops—and stops.
Lo, the wild swan had deserted,
  And a rat had gnawed the reeds.

XVII

Ellie went home sad and slow.
If she found the lover ever,
  With his red-roan steed of steeds,
  Sooth I know not! but I know
She could never show him—never,
  That swan's nest among the reeds!

THE CRY OF THE HUMAN

I

'There is no God,' the foolish saith,
　　But none 'There is no sorrow,'
And nature oft the cry of faith
　　In bitter need will borrow:
Eyes, which the preacher could not school,
　　By wayside graves are raisèd,
And lips say 'God be pitiful,'
　　Who ne'er said 'God be praisèd.'
　　　　　　　　　Be pitiful, O God!

II

The tempest stretches from the steep
　　The shadow of its coming,
The beasts grow tame, and near us creep,
　　As help were in the human;
Yet, while the cloud-wheels roll and grind,
　　We spirits tremble under!—
The hills have echoes, but we find
　　No answer for the thunder.
　　　　　　　　　Be pitiful, O God!

III

The battle hurtles on the plains,
　　Earth feels new scythes upon her;
We reap our brothers for the wains,
　　And call the harvest—honour;
Draw face to face, front line to line,
　　One image all inherit,—
Then kill, curse on, by that same sign,
　　Clay, clay,—and spirit, spirit.
　　　　　　　　　Be pitiful, O God!

IV

The plague runs festering through the town,
   And never a bell is tolling,
And corpses, jostled 'neath the moon,
   Nod to the dead-cart's rolling.
The young child calleth for the cup,
   The strong man brings it weeping;
The mother from her babe looks up,
   And shieks away its sleeping.
                     Be pitiful, O God!

V

The plague of gold strikes far and near,
   And deep and strong it enters;
This purple chimar which we wear
   Makes madder than the centaur's:
Our thoughts grow blank, our words grow strange,
   We cheer the pale gold-diggers—
Each soul is worth so much on 'Change,
   And marked, like sheep, with figures.
                     Be pitiful, O God!

VI

The curse of gold upon the land
   The lack of bread enforces;
The rail-cars snort from strand to strand,
   Like more of Death's white horses!
The rich preach 'rights' and future days,
   And hear no angel scoffing,—
The poor die mute—with starving gaze
   On corn-ships in the offing.
                     Be pitiful, O God!

VII

We meet together at the feast,
  To private mirth betake us;
We stare down in the winecup, lest
  Some vacant chair should shake us.
We name delight, and pledge it round—
  'It shall be ours to-morrow!'
God's seraphs, do your voices sound
  As sad in naming sorrow?
                    Be pitiful, O God!

VIII

We sit together, with the skies,
  The steadfast skies, above us,
We look into each other's eyes,
  'And how long will you love us?'—
The eyes grow dim with prophecy,
  The voices, low and breathless,—
'Till death us part!'—O words, to be
  Our *best*, for love the deathless!
                    Be pitiful, O God!

IX

We tremble by the harmless bed
  Of one loved and departed:
Our tears drop on the lips that said
  Last night, 'Be stronger-hearted!'
O God,—to clasp those fingers close,
  And yet to feel so lonely!—
To see a light upon such brows,
  Which is the daylight only!
                    Be pitiful, O God!

X

The happy children come to us,
　And look up in our faces:
They ask us—Was it thus, and thus,
　When we were in their places?—
We cannot speak;—we see anew
　The hills we used to live in,
And feel our mother's smile press through
　The kisses she is giving.
　　　　　　　　　　Be pitiful, O God!

XI

We pray together at the kirk,
　For mercy, mercy, solely:
Hands weary with the evil work,
　We lift them to the Holy.
The corpse is calm below our knee,
　Its spirit, bright before Thee—
Between them, worse than either, we—
　Without the rest of glory!
　　　　　　　　　　Be pitiful, O God!

XII

We leave the communing of men,
　The murmur of the passions,
And live alone, to live again
　With endless generations.
Are we so brave?—The sea and sky
　In silence lift their mirrors,
And, glassed therein, our spirits high
　Recoil from their own terrors.
　　　　　　　　　　Be pitiful, O God!

XIII

We sit on hills our childhood wist,
　　Woods, hamlets, streams, beholding:
The sun strikes through the farthest mist,
　　The city's spire to golden.
The city's golden spire it was,
　　When hope and health were strongest,
But now it is the churchyard grass
　　We look upon the longest.
　　　　　　　　　Be pitiful, O God!

XIV

And soon all vision waxeth dull—
　　Men whisper, 'He is dying':
We cry no more 'Be pitiful!'
　　We have no strength for crying.
No strength, no need. Then, soul of mine,
　　Look up and triumph rather—
Lo, in the depth of God's Divine,
　　The Son adjures the Father,
　　　　　BE PITIFUL, O GOD!

THE CRY OF THE CHILDREN

Do ye hear the children weeping, O my brothers,
    Ere the sorrow comes with years?
They are leaning their young heads against their mothers,
    And *that* cannot stop their tears.
The young lambs are bleating in the meadows,
    The young birds are chirping in the nest,
The young fawns are playing with the shadows,
    The young flowers are blowing toward the west—
But the young, young children, O my brothers,
    They are weeping bitterly!
They are weeping in the playtime of the others,
    In the country of the free.

II

Do you question the young children in the sorrow
    Why their tears are falling so?
The old man may weep for his to-morrow
    Which is lost in Long Ago;
The old tree is leafless in the forest,
    The old year is ending in the frost,
The old wound, if stricken, is the sorest,
    The old hope is hardest to be lost.
But the young, young children, O my brothers,
    Do you ask them why they stand
Weeping sore before the bosoms of their mothers,
    In our happy Fatherland?

III

They look up with their pale and sunken faces,
  And their looks are sad to see,
For the man's hoary anguish draws and presses
  Down the cheeks of infancy.
'Your old earth,' they say, 'is very dreary;
  Our young feet,' they say, 'are very weak!
Few paces have we taken, yet are weary—
  Our grave-rest is very far to seek.
Ask the aged why they weep, and not the children;
  For the outside earth is cold;
And we young ones stand without, in our bewildering,
  And the graves are for the old.'

'True,' say the children, 'it may happen
  That we die before our time;
Little Alice died last year—her grave is shapen
  Like a snowball, in the rime.
We looked into the pit prepared to take her:
  Was no room for any work in the close clay!
From the sleep wherein she lieth none will wake her,
  Crying, "Get up, little Alice! it is day."
If you listen by that grave, in sun and shower,
  With your ear down, little Alice never cries;
Could we see her face, be sure we should not know her,
  For the smile has time for growing in her eyes:
And merry go her moments, lulled and stilled in
  The shroud by the kirk-chime.
'It is good when it happens,' say the children,
  'That we die before our time.'

Alas, alas, the children! they are seeking
    Death in life, as best to have;
They are binding up their hearts away from breaking,
    With a cerement from the grave.
Go out, children, from the mine and from the city,
    Sing out, children, as the little thrushes do;
Pluck you handfuls of the meadow-cowslips pretty,
    Laugh aloud, to feel your fingers let them through!
But they answer, 'Are your cowslips of the meadows
    Like our weeds anear the mine?
Leave us quiet in the dark of the coal-shadows,
    From your pleasures fair and fine!

VI

'For oh,' say the children, 'we are weary,
    And we cannot run or leap;
If we cared for any meadows, it were merely
    To drop down in them and sleep.
Our knees tremble sorely in the stooping,
    We fall upon our faces, trying to go;
And, underneath our heavy eyelids drooping,
    The reddest flower would look as pale as snow;
For, all day, we drag our burden tiring
    Through the coal-dark, underground—
Or, all day, we drive the wheels of iron
    In the factories, round and round.

VII

'For all day, the wheels are droning, turning;
　　　Their wind comes in our faces,—
Till our hearts turn,—our heads with pulses burning,
　　　And the walls turn in their places:
Turns the sky in the high window blank and reeling,
　　Turns the long light that drops adown the wall,
Turn the black flies that crawl along the ceiling,
　　All are turning, all the day, and we with all.
And all day, the iron wheels are droning,
　　　And sometimes we could pray,
"O ye wheels," (breaking out in a mad moaning)
　　　"Stop! be silent for to-day!"'

VIII

Aye, be silent! Let them hear each other breathing
　　　For a moment, mouth to mouth!
Let them touch each other's hands, in a fresh wreathing
　　　Of their tender human youth!
Let them feel that this cold metallic motion
　　Is not all the life God fashions or reveals:
Let them prove their living souls against the notion
　　That they live in you, or under you, O wheels!—
Still, all day, the iron wheels go onward,
　　　Grinding life down from its mark;
And the children's souls, which God is calling sunward,
　　　Spin on blindly in the dark.

IX

Now tell the poor young children, O my brothers,
    To look up to Him and pray;
So the blessed One who blesseth all the others,
    Will bless them another day.
They answer, 'Who is God that He should hear us,
    While the rushing of the iron wheels is stirred?
When we sob aloud, the human creatures near us
    Pass by, hearing not, or answer not a word.
And *we* hear not (for the wheels in their resounding)
    Strangers speaking at the door:
Is it likely God, with angels singing round him,
    Hears our weeping any more?

X

'Two words, indeed, of praying we remember,
    And at midnight's hour of harm,
"Our Father," looking upward in the chamber,
    We say softly for a charm.
We know no other words except "Our Father,"
    And we think that, in some pause of angels' song,
God may pluck them with the silence sweet to gather,
    And hold both within His right hand which is strong.
"Our Father!" If He heard us, He would surely
    (For they call Him good and mild)
Answer, smiling down the steep world very purely,
    "Come and rest with Me, My child."'

XI

'But no!' say the children, weeping faster,
    'He is speechless as a stone:
And they tell us, of His image is the master
    Who commands us to work on.
Go to!' say the children,—'up in heaven,
    Dark, wheel-like, turning clouds are all we find.
Do not mock us; grief has made us unbelieving—
    We look up for God, but tears have made us blind.'
Do you hear the children weeping and disproving,
    O my brothers, what ye preach?
For God's possible is taught by His world's loving,
    And the children doubt of each.

XII

And well may the children weep before you!
    They are weary ere they run;
They have never seen the sunshine, nor the glory
    Which is brighter than the sun.
They know the grief of man, without its wisdom;
    They sink in man's despair, without its calm;
Are slaves, without the liberty in Christdom,
    Are martyrs, by the pang without the palm,—
Are worn as if with age, yet unretrievingly
    The harvest of its memories cannot reap,—
Are orphans of the earthly love and heavenly.
    Let them weep! let them weep!

They look up with their pale and sunken faces,
    And their look is dread to see,
For they mind you of their angels in high places,
    With eyes turned on Deity!—
'How long,' they say, 'how long, O cruel nation,
    Will you stand, to move the world, on a child's heart,—
Stifle down with a mailed heel its palpitation,
    And tread onward to your throne amid the mart?
Our blood splashes upward, O gold-heaper,
    And your purple shows your path!
But the child's sob in the silence curses deeper
    Than the strong man in his wrath.'

THE POET AND THE BIRD

A FABLE

I

Said a people to a poet—'Go out from
    among us straightway!
While we are thinking earthly things,
    thou singest of divine.
There's a little fair brown nightingale,
    who, sitting in the gateway,
Makes fitter music to our ear than any
    song of thine!'

II

The poet went out weeping—the nightin-
    gale ceased chanting,
  'Now, wherefore, O thou nightingale,
    is all thy sweetness done?'
—'I cannot sing my earthly things, the
    heavenly poet wanting,
  Whose highest harmony includes the
    lowest under sun.'

III

The poet went out weeping,—and died
    abroad, bereft there:
  The bird flew to his grave and died
    amid a thousand wails.
And, when I last came by the place,
    I swear the music left there
  Was only of the poet's song, and not
    the nightingale's.

Poems Selected from

POEMS

2 volumes
(new edition, 1850)

Preface

This collection included all the poems which had already been published in the volumes of 1844, twenty-seven of those which appeared with "The Seraphim" in 1838, and none at all from the earlier work.

The most remarkable of the new poems were the *Sonnets from the Portuguese*, a squence of love poems which Elizabeth Barrett had written to Robert Browning during their courtship, but which she had not shown to him until three years after their marriage. They were hardly noticed at the time but have excited enthusiastic comment ever since. Robert Browning himself throught some of these sonnets were as good as Shakespeare's.

There were several poems in these volumes which Elizabeth Barrett Browning feared would offend her father. She had completed them, and sent them to *Blackwood's*, just before she left England after her secret marriage in September 1846. She worried that her father, reading them in this context, might find them offensive—"A Woman's Shortcomings", "A Man's Requirements" and "Change upon Change" developed the theme of the worthlessness of love unless it can forgive all and remain eternal. Her father had loved her but, when she married, had said he never wanted to see her again which, to her, cast doubts on the nature of such "love". "Confessions", although not written until after she was in Italy, was even more likely to offend her father—the seventh stanza sounds very much as though it were written with Mr. Barrett in mind.

At least the clearly autobiographical "Hector in the Garden" could cause no distress, describing so charmingly as it does her childhood home, Hope End. Nor could the sonnet to Flush, the spaniel sent to her in 1841 while she was still in Torquay suffering from the effects of her brother's death. Flush was her constant companion until his death in 1855. This poem was one of three tributes written to her dog.

"Hiram Powers' Greek Slave" offended some critics (Coventry Patmore for example) with its imagery. Hiram Powers, the American sculptor, was a friend of the Brownings whom they met in Florence where he also lived. They visited his studio often. The statue of the poem was shown at the International Exhibition in London in 1851. Elizabeth Barrett Browning admired it but expressed here her doubts that art should in any way appear to sanctify evil.

A SABBATH MORNING AT SEA

I

The ship went on with solemn face;
   To meet the darkness on the deep,
     The solemn ship went onward.
I bowed down weary in the place,
   For parting tears and present sleep
     Had weighed mine eyelids down-
       ward.

II

Thick sleep which shut all dreams from me,
   And kept my inner self apart
     And quiet from emotion,
Then brake away and left me free,
   Made conscious of a human heart
     Betwixt the heaven and ocean.

III

The new sight, the new wondrous sight!
   The waters round me, turbulent,—
     The skies impassive o'er me,
Calm, in a moonless, sunless light,
   Half glorified by that intent
     Of holding the day-glory!

IV

Two pale thin clouds did stand upon
   The meeting line of sea and sky,
     With aspect still and mystic.
I think they did foresee the sun,
   And rested on their prophecy
     In quietude majestic,

V

Then flushed to radiance where they stood,
    Like statues by the open tomb
        Of shining saints half risen.—
The sun!—he came up to be viewed,
    And sky and sea made mighty room
        To inaugurate the vision.

VI

I oft had seen the dawnlight run,
    As red wine, through the hills, and break
        Through many a mist's inurning;
But, here, no earth profaned the sun!
    Heaven, ocean, did alone partake
        The sacrament of morning.

VII

Away with thoughts fantastical!
    I would be humble to my worth,
        Self-guarded as self-doubted:
Though here no earthly shadows fall,
    I, joying, grieving without earth,
        May desecrate without it.

VIII

God's sabbath morning sweeps the waves;
    I would not praise the pageant high,
        Yet miss the dedicature.
I, carried toward the sunless graves
    By force of natural things,—should I
        Exult in only nature?

IX

And could I bear to sit alone
  'Mid nature's fixed benignities,
    While my warm pulse was moving?
Too dark thou art, O glittering sun,
  Too strait ye are, capacious seas,
    To satisfy the loving!

X

It seems a better lot than so,
  To sit with friends beneath the beech,
    And feel them dear and dearer;
Or follow children as they go
  In pretty pairs, with softened speech,
    As the church-bells ring nearer.

XI

Love me, sweet friends, this sabbath day!
  The sea sings round me while ye roll
    Afar the hymn unaltered,
And kneel, where once I knelt to pray,
  And bless me deeper in the soul,
    Because the voice has faltered.

XII

And though this sabbath comes to me
  Without the stolèd minister
    Or chanting congregation,
God's spirit brings communion, HE
  Who brooded soft on waters drear,
    Creator on creation.

XIII

Himself, I think, shall draw me higher,
    Where keep the saints with harp and song
      An endless sabbath morning,
And on that sea commixed with fire
    Oft drop their eyelids, raised too long
      To the full Godhead's burning.

HUMAN LIFE'S MYSTERY

I

We sow the glebe, we reap the corn,
    We build the house where we may rest,
And then, at moments, suddenly,
We look up to the great wide sky,
Inquiring wherefore we were born . . .
    For earnest, or for jest?

II

The senses folding thick and dark
    About the stifled soul within,
We guess diviner things beyond,
And yearn to them with yearning fond;
We strike out blindly to a mark
    Believed in, but not seen.

III

We vibrate to the pant and thrill
    Wherewith Eternity has curled
In serpent-twine about God's seat;
While, freshening upward to His feet,
In gradual growth His full-leaved will
    Expands from world to world.

IV

And, in the tumult and excess
  Of act and passion under sun,
We sometimes hear—oh, soft and far,
As silver star did touch with star,
The kiss of Peace and Righteousness
  Through all things that are done.

V

God keeps His holy mysteries
  Just on the outside of man's dream.
In diapason slow, we think
To hear their pinions rise and sink,
While they float pure beneath His eyes,
  Like swans adown a stream.

VI

Abstractions, are they, from the forms
  Of His great beauty?—exaltations
From His great glory?—strong previsions
Of what we shall be?—intuitions
Of what we are—in calms and storms,
  Beyond our peace and passions?

VII

Things nameless! which, in passing so,
  Do stroke us with a subtle grace.
We say, 'Who passes?'—they are dumb.
We cannot see them go or come:
Their touches fall soft—cold—as snow
  Upon a blind man's face.

VIII

Yet, touching so, they draw above
　Our common thoughts to Heaven's
　　unknown;
Our daily joy and pain, advance
To a divine significance,—
Our human love—O mortal love,
　That light is not its own!

IX

And, sometimes, horror chills our blood
　To be so near such mystic Things,
And we wrap round us, for defence.
Our purple manners, moods of sense—
As angels, from the face of God,
　Stand hidden in their wings.

X

And, sometimes, through life's heavy swound
　We grope for them!—with strangled breath
We stretch our hands abroad and try
To reach them in our agony.—
And widen, so, the broad life-wound
　Which soon is large enough for death.

QUESTION AND ANSWER

I

Love you seek for, presupposes
   Summer heat and sunny glow.
Tell me, do you find moss-roses
   Budding, blooming in the snow?
Snow might kill the rose-tree's root—
Shake it quickly from your foot,
   Lest it harm you as you go.

II

From the ivy where it dapples
   A grey ruin, stone by stone,—
Do you look for grapes or apples,
   Or for sad green leaves alone?
Pluck the leaves off, two or three—
Keep them for morality
   When you shall be safe and gone.

CHANGE UPON CHANGE

I

Five months ago the stream did flow,
   The lilies bloomed within the sedge,
And we were lingering to and fro,
Where none will track thee in this snow,
   Along the stream beside the hedge.
Ah, Sweet, be free to love and go!
   For if I do not hear thy foot,
   The frozen river is as mute,
   The flowers have dried down to the root.
And why, since these be changed since May,
   Shouldst *thou* change less than *they*?

And slow, slow as the winter snow
   The tears have drifted to mine eyes;
And my poor cheeks, five months ago
Set blushing at thy praises so,
   Put paleness on for a disguise.
Ah Sweet, be free to praise and go!
   For if my face is turned too pale,
   It was thine oath that first did fail,—
   It was thy love proved false and frail!
   And why, since these be changed enow,
      Should *I* change less than *thou*?

A WOMAN'S SHORTCOMINGS

I

She has laughed as softly as if she sighed,
   She has counted six, and over,
Of a purse well filled and a heart well tried—
   Oh, each a worthy lover!
They 'give her time;' for her soul must slip
   Where the world has set the grooving.
She will lie to none with her fair red lip,—
   But love seeks truer loving.

II

She trembles her fan in a sweetness dumb,
   As her thoughts were beyond recalling,
With a glance for *one*, and a glance for *some*,
   From her eyelids rising and falling;
Speaks common words with a blushful air,
   Hears bold words, unreproving;
But her silence says—what she never will swear—
   And love seeks better loving.

III

Go, lady, lean to the night-guitar
   And drop a smile to the bringer,
Then smile as sweetly, when he is far,
   At the voice of an in-door singer.
Bask tenderly beneath tender eyes;
   Glance lightly, on their removing;
And join new vows to old perjuries—
   But dare not call it loving.

IV

Unless you can think, when the song is done,
   No other is soft in the rhythm;
Unless you can feel, when left by One,
   That all men else go with him;
Unless you can know, when unpraised by his breath,
   That your beauty itself wants proving;
Unless you can swear 'For life, for death!'—
   Oh, fear to call it loving!

V

Unless you can muse in a crowd all day
   On the absent face that fixed you;
Unless you can love, as the angels may,
   With the breadth of heaven betwixt you;
Unless you can dream that his faith is fast,
   Through behoving and unbehoving;
Unless you can *die* when the dream is past—
   Oh, never call it loving!

THE MASK

I

I have a smiling face, she said,
    I have a jest for all I meet,
I have a garland for my head
    And all its flowers are sweet,—
And so you call me gay, she said.

II

Grief taught to me this smile, she said,
    And Wrong did teach this jesting bold;
These flowers were plucked from garden-bed
    While a death-chime was tolled.
And what now will you say?—she said.

III

Behind no prison-grate, she said,
    Which slurs the sunshine half a mile
Live captives so uncomforted
    As souls behind a smile.
God's pity let us pray, she said.

IV

I know my face is bright, she said,—
    Such brightness, dying suns diffuse;
I bear upon my forehead shed
    The sign of what I lose,—
The ending of my day, she said.

V

If I dared leave this smile, she said,
    And take a moan upon my mouth,
And tie a cypress round my head,
    And let my tears run smooth,—
It were the happier way, she said.

And since that must not be, she said,
  I fain your bitter world would leave.
How calmly, calmly, smile the Dead,
  Who do not, therefore, grieve!
The yea of Heaven is yea, she said.

VII

But in your bitter world, she said,
  Face-joy's a costly mask to wear.
'Tis bought with pangs long nourishèd,
  And rounded to despair.
Grief's earnest makes life's play, she said.

VIII

Ye weep for those who weep? she said—
  Ah fools! I bid you pass them by.
Go, weep for those whose hearts have bled
  What time their eyes were dry.
Whom sadder can I say? she said.

A MAN'S REQUIREMENTS

I

Love me, Sweet, with all thou art,
  Feeling, thinking, seeing,—
Love me in the lightest part,
  Love me in full being.

II

Love me with thine open youth
  In its frank surrender;
With the vowing of thy mouth,
  With its silence tender.

III

Love me with thin azure eyes,
    Made for earnest granting,
Taking colour from the skies,
    Can Heaven's truth be wanting?

IV

Love me with their lids, that fall
    Snow-like at first meeting;
Love me with thine heart, that all
    Neighbours then see beating.

V

Love me with thine hand stretched out
    Freely—open-minded;
Love me with thy loitering foot,—
    Hearing one behind it.

VI

Love me with thy voice, that turns
    Sudden faint above me;
Love me with thy blush that burns
    When I murmur, *Love me!*

VII

Love me with thy thinking soul,
    Break it to love-sighing;
Love me with thy thoughts that roll
    On through living—dying.

VIII

Love me in thy gorgeous airs,
    When the world has crowned thee!
Love me, kneeling at thy prayers,
    With the angels round thee.

IX

Love me pure, as musers do,
   Up the woodlands shady;
Love me gaily, fast and true,
   As a winsome lady.

X

Through all hopes that keep us brave,
   Further off or nigher,
Love me for the house and grave,—
   And for something higher.

XI

Thus, if thou wilt prove me, Dear,
   Woman's love no fable,
I will love *thee*—half a year—
   As a man is able.

A DENIAL

I

We have met late—it is too late to meet,
   O friend, not more than friend!
Death's forecome shroud is tangled round my feet,
And if I step or stir, I touch the end.
   In this last jeopardy
Can I approach thee, I, who cannot move?
How shall I answer thy request for love?
   Look in my face and see.

II

I love thee not, I dare not love thee! go
    In silence; drop my hand.
If thou seek roses, seek them where they blow
In garden-alleys, not in desert-sand.
    Can life and death agree,
That thou shouldst stoop thy song to my complaint?
I cannot love thee. If the word is faint,
    Look in my face and see.

III

I might have loved thee in some former days.
    Oh, then, my spirits had leapt
As now they sink, at hearing thy love-praise.
Before these faded cheeks were overwept,
    Had this been asked of me,
To love thee with my whole strong heart and head,—
I should have said still . . . yes, but *smiled* and said,
    'Look in my face and see!'

IV

But now . . . God sees me, God, who took my heart
    And drowned it in life's surge.
In all your wide warm earth I have no part—
A light song overcomes me like a dirge.
    Could Love's great harmony
The saints keep step to when their bonds are loose,
Not weigh me down? am *I* a wife to choose?
    Look in my face and see.

V

While I behold, as plain as one who dreams,
  Some woman of full worth,
Whose voice, as cadenced as a silver stream's,
Shall prove the fountain-soul which sends it forth;
  One younger, more thought-free
And fair and gay, than I, thou must forget,
With brighter eyes than these . . . which are not wet . . .
  Look in my face and see!

VI

So farewell thou, whom I have known too late
  To let thee come so near.
Be counted happy while men call thee great,
And one belovèd woman feels thee dear!—
  Not I!—that cannot be.
I am lost, I am changed,—I must go farther, where
The change shall take me worse, and no one dare
  Look in my face to see.

VII

Meantime I bless thee. By these thoughts of mine
  I bless thee from all such!
I bless thy lamp to oil, thy cup to wine,
Thy hearth to joy, thy hand to an equal touch
  Of loyal troth. For me,
I love thee not, I love thee not!—away!
Here's no more courage in my soul to say
  'Look in my face and see.'

A REED

I

I am no trumpet, but a reed:
No flattering breath shall from me lead
   A silver sound, a hollow sound:
I will not ring, for priest or king,
One blast that in re-echoing
   Would leave a bondsman faster bound.

II

I am no trumpet, but a reed,—
A broken reed, the wind indeed
   Left flat upon a dismal shore;
Yet if a little maid or child
Should sigh within it, earnest-mild
   This reed will answer evermore.

III

I am no trumpet, but a reed.
Go, tell the fishers, as they spread
   Their nets along the river's edge,
I will not tear their nets at all,
Nor pierce their hands, if they should fall;
   Then let them leave me in the sedge.

HECTOR IN THE GARDEN

I

Nine years old! The first of any
    Seem the happiest years that come:
    Yet when *I* was nine, I said
    No such word!—I thought instead
That the Greeks had used as many
    In besieging Ilium.

II

Nine green years had scarcely brought me
    To my childhood's haunted spring:
    I had life, like flowers and bees,
    In betwixt the country trees.
And the sun the pleasure taught me
    Which he teacheth every thing.

III

If the rain fell, there was sorrow,
    Little head leant on the pane,
    Little finger drawing down it
    The long trailing drops upon it,
And the 'Rain, rain, come to-morrow,'
    Said for charm against the rain.

IV

Such a charm was right Canidian,
    Though you meet it with a jeer!
    If I said it long enough,
    Then the rain hummed dimly off,
And the thrush with his pure Lydian
    Was left only to the ear;

V

And the sun and I together
  Went a-rushing out of doors!
  We, our tender spirits, drew
  Over hill and dale in view,
Glimmering hither, glimmering thither,
  In the footsteps of the showers.

VI

Underneath the chestnuts dripping,
  Through the grasses wet and fair,
  Straight I sought my garden-ground
  With the laurel on the mound,
And the pear-tree oversweeping
  A side-shadow of green air.

VII

In the garden lay supinely
  A huge giant wrought of spade!
  Arms and legs were stretched at length
  In a passive giant strength,—
The fine meadow turf, cut finely,
  Round them laid and interlaid.

VIII

Call him Hector, son of Priam!
  Such his title and degree:
  With my rake I smoothed his brow,
  Both his cheeks I weeded through,
But a rimer such as I am
  Scarce can sing his dignity.

IX

Eyes of gentianellas azure,
　　Staring, winking at the skies;
　　Nose of gillyflowers and box;
　　Scented grasses put for locks,
Which a little breeze, at pleasure,
　　Set a-waving round his eyes.

X

Brazen helm of daffodillies,
　　With a glitter toward the light;
　　Purple violets for the mouth,
　　Breathing perfumes west and south;
And a sword of flashing lilies,
　　Holden ready for the fight.

XI

And a breastplate made of daisies,
　　Closely fitting, leaf on leaf;
　　Periwinkles interlaced
　　Drawn for belt about the waist;
While the brown bees, humming praises,
　　Shot their arrows round the chief.

XII

And who knows (I sometimes wondered)
　　If the disembodied soul
　　Of old Hector, once of Troy,
　　Might not take a dreary joy
Here to enter—if it thundered,
　　Rolling up the thunder-roll?

Rolling this way from Troy-ruin,
   In this body rude and rife
   Just to enter, and take rest
   'Neath the daisies of the breast—
They, with tender roots, renewing
   His heroic heart to life?

XIV

Who could know? I sometimes started
   At a motion or a sound!
   Did his mouth speak—naming Troy,
   With an ὀτοτοτοτοῖ?
Did the pulse of the Strong-hearted
   Make the daisies tremble round?

XV

It was hard to answer, often:
   But the birds sang in the tree—
   But the little birds sang bold
   In the pear-tree green and old,
And my terror seemed to soften
   Through the courage of their glee.

XVI

Oh, the birds, the tree, the ruddy
   And white blossoms, sleek with rain!
   Oh, my garden, rich with pansies!
   Oh, my childhood's bright romances!
All revive, like Hector's body,
   And I see them stir again!

XVII

And despite life's changes—chances,
   And despite the deathbell's toll,
They press on me in full seeming!
   Help, some angel! stay this dreaming!
As the birds sang in the branches,
   Sing God's patience through my soul!

XVIII

That no dreamer, no neglecter
   Of the present's work unsped,
I may wake up and be doing,
   Life's heroic ends pursuing,
Though my past is dead as Hector,
   And though Hector is twice dead.

FLUSH OR FAUNUS

You see this dog. It was but yesterday
I mused forgetful of his presence here
Till thought on thought drew downward tear on tear,
When from the pillow where wet-cheeked I lay,
A head as hairy as Faunus thrust its way
Right sudden against my face,—two golden-clear
Great eyes astonished mine,—a drooping ear
Did flap me on either cheek to dry the spray!
I started first as some Arcadian
Amazed by goatly god in twilight grove,
But as the bearded vision closelier ran
My tears off, I knew Flush, and rose above
Surprise and sadness,—thanking the true PAN
Who, by low creatures, leads to heights of love.

HIRAM POWERS' GREEK SLAVE

They say Ideal beauty cannot enter
The house of anguish. On the threshold stands
An alien Image with enshackled hands,
Called the Greek Slave! as if the artist meant her
(That passionless perfection which he lent her,
Shadowed not darkened where the sill expands)
To, so, confront man's crimes in different lands
With man's ideal sense. Pierce to the centre,
Art's fiery finger!—and break up ere long
The serfdom of this world! appeal, fair stone,
From God's pure heights of beauty against man's wrong!
Catch up in thy divine face, not alone
East griefs but west,—and strike and shame the strong,
By thunders of white silence, overthrown.

CONFESSIONS

I

Face to face in my chamber, my silent
　　　　chamber, I saw her:
God and she and I only, . . there, I sate
　　　　down to draw her
Soul through the clefts of confession . . .
　　　　Speak, I am holding thee fast,
As the angels of resurrection shall do it
　　　　at the last.
　　　　'My cup is blood-red
　　　　With my sin,' she said,
　　'And I pour it out to the bitter lees,
As if the angels of judgement stood over
　　　　me strong at the last,
　　　Or as thou wert as these!'

II

When God smote His hands together,
    and struck out thy soul as a spark
Into the organized glory of things, from
    deeps of the dark,—
Say, didst thou shine, didst thou burn,
    didst thou honour the power in the form,
As the star does at night, or the fire-fly,
    or even the little ground-worm?
    'I have sinned,' she said,
    'For my seed-light shed
Has smouldered away from His first
    decrees!
The cypress praiseth the fire-fly, the
    ground-leaf praiseth the worm,—
    I am viler than these!'

III

When God on that sin had pity, and
    did not trample thee straight
With His wild rains beating and drench-
    ing thy light found inadequate;
When He only sent thee the north-
    winds, a little searching and chill,
To quicken thy flame . . didst thou kindle
    and flash to the heights of His will?
    'I have sinned,' she said,
    'Unquickened, unspread
My fire dropt down, and I wept on
    my knees!
I only said of His winds of the north as
    I shrank from their chill, . .
    What delight is in these?'

IV

When God on that sin had pity, and did
      not meet it as such,
But tempered the wind to thy uses, and
      softened the world to thy touch,
At least thou wast moved in thy soul,
      though unable to prove it afar,
Thou couldst carry thy light like a jewel,
      not giving it out like a star?
     'I have sinned,' she said,
     'And not merited
The gift He gives, by the grace He sees!
The mine-cave praiseth the jewel, the
      hillside praiseth the star;
   I am viler than these.'

V

Then I cried aloud in my passion, . .
      Unthankful and impotent creature,
To throw up thy scorn unto God through
      the rents in thy beggarly nature!
If He, the all-giving and loving, is
      served so unduly, what then
Hast thou done to the weak and the false,
      and the changing, . . thy fellows of men?
     'I have *loved*,' she said,
     (Words bowing her head
As the wind the wet acacia-trees!)
'I saw God sitting above me,—but I . . .
      I sate among men,
   And I have loved these.'

VI

Again with a lifted voice, like a choral
        trumpet that takes
The lowest note of a viol that trembles,
        and triumphing breaks
On the air with it solemn and clear,—
        'Behold! I have sinned not in this!
Where I loved, I have loved much and
        well,—I have verily loved not amiss.
        Let the living,' she said,
        'Inquire of the Dead,
In the house of the pale-fronted Images:
My own true dead will answer for me,
        that I have not loved amiss
        In my love for all these.

'The least touch of their hands in the
        morning, I keep it by day and by night;
Their least step on the stair, at the door.
        still throbs through me, if ever so light;
Their least gift, which they left to my
        childhood, far off, in the long-ago years,
Is now turned from a toy to a relic, and
        seen through the crystals of tears.
        Dig the snow,' she said,
        'For my churchyard bed,
Yet I, as I sleep, shall not fear to freeze.
If one only of these my beloveds, shall
        love me with heart-warm tears,
        As I have loved these!

VIII

'If I angered any among them, from
            thenceforth my own life was sore;
If I fell by chance from their presence,
            I clung to their memory more.
Their tender I often felt holy, their
            bitter I sometimes called sweet;
And whenever their heart has refused
            me, I fell down straight at their feet,
        I have loved,' she said,—
        'Man is weak, God is dread,
     Yet the weak man dies with his spirit at ease,
Having poured such an unguent of love
            but once on the Saviour's feet,
        As I lavished for these.'

IX

'Go,' I cried, 'thou hast chosen the
            Human, and left the Divine!
Then, at least, have the Human shared
            with thee their wild berry-wine?
Have they loved back thy love, and
            when strangers approached thee with blame,
Have they covered thy fault with their
            kisses, and loved thee the same?'
        But she shrunk and said,
        'God, over my head,
   Must sweep in the wrath of his judgement-seas,
If *He* shall deal with me sinning, but
            only indeed the same
        And no gentler than these.'

Sonnets from the Portuguese

I

I thought once how Theocritus had sung
Of the sweet years, the dear and wished-for years,
Who each one in a gracious hand appears
To bear a gift for mortals, old or young:
And, as I mused it in his antique tongue,
I saw, in gradual vision through my tears,
The sweet, sad years, the melancholy years,
Those of my own life, who by turns had flung
A shadow across me. Straightway I was 'ware,
So weeping, how a mystic Shape did move
Behind me, and drew me backward by the hair;
And a voice said in mastery, while I strove,—
'Guess now who holds thee?'—'Death,' I said. But,
     there,
The silver answer rang,—'Not Death, but Love.'

II

But only three in all God's universe
Have heard this word thou hast said,—Himself, beside
Thee speaking, and me listening! and replied
One of us . . . *that* was God, . . . and laid the curse
So darkly on my eyelids, as to amerce
My sight from seeing thee,—that if I had died,
The death-weights, placed there, would have signified
Less absolute exclusion. 'Nay' is worse
From God than from all others, O my friend!
Men could not part us with their worldly jars,
Nor the seas change us, nor the tempests bend;
Our hands would touch for all the mountain-bars.—
And, heaven being rolled between us at the end,
We should but vow the faster for the stars.

III

Unlike are we, unlike, O princely Heart!
Unlike our uses and our destinies.
Our ministering two angels look surprise
On one another, as they strike athwart
Their wings in passing. Thou, bethink thee, art
A guest for queens to social pageantries,
With gages from a hundred brighter eyes
Than tears even can make mine, to play thy part
Of chief musician. What hast *thou* to do
With looking from the lattice-lights at me,
A poor, tired, wandering singer, . . . singing through
The dark, and leaning up a cypress tree?
The chrism is on thine head,—on mine, the dew,—
And Death must dig the level where these agree.

IV

Thou hast thy calling to some palace-floor,
Most gracious singer of high poems! where
The dancers will break footing, from the care
Of watching up thy pregnant lips for more.
And dost thou lift this house's latch too poor
For hand of thine? and canst thou think and bear
To let thy music drop here unaware
In folds of golden fulness at my door?
Look up and see the casement broken in,
The bats and owlets builders in the roof!
My cricket chirps against thy mandolin.
Hush, call no echo up in further proof
Of desolation! there's a voice within
That weeps . . . as thou must sing . . . alone, aloof.

V

I lift my heavy heart up solemnly,
As once Electra her sepulchral urn,
And, looking in thine eyes, I overturn
The ashes at thy feet. Behold and see
What a great heap of grief lay hid in me,
And how the red wild sparkles dimly burn
Through the ashen greyness. If thy foot in scorn
Could tread them out to darkness utterly,
It might be well perhaps. But if instead
Thou wait beside me for the wind to blow
The grey dust up, . . . those laurels on thine head,
O my Belovëd, will not shield thee so,
That none of all the fires shall scorch and shred
The hair beneath. Stand further off then! go.

VI

Go from me. Yet I feel that I shall stand
Henceforward in thy shadow. Nevermore
Alone upon the threshold of my door
Of individual life, I shall command
The uses of my soul, nor lift my hand
Serenely in the sunshine as before,
Without the sense of that which I forbore—
Thy touch upon the palm. The widest land
Doom takes to part us, leaves thy heart in mine
With pulses that beat double. What I do
And what I dream include thee, as the wine
Must taste of its own grapes. And when I sue
God for myself, He hears that name of thine,
And sees within my eyes the tears of two.

VII

The face of all the world is changed, I think,
Since first I heard the footsteps of thy soul
Move still, oh, still, beside me, as they stole
Betwixt me and the dreadful outer brink
Of obvious death, where I, who thought to sink,
Was caught up into love, and taught the whole
Of life in a new rhythm. The cup of dole
God gave for baptism, I am fain to drink,
And praise its sweetness, Sweet, with thee anear.
The names of country, heaven, are changed away
For where thou art or shalt be, there or here;
And this . . . this lute and song . . . loved yesterday
(The singing angels know) are only dear
Because thy name moves right in what they say.

VIII

What can I give thee back, O liberal
And princely giver, who hast brought the gold
And purple of thine heart, unstained, untold,
And laid them on the outside of the wall
For such as I to take or leave withal,
In unexpected largesse? am I cold,
Ungrateful, that for these most manifold
High gifts, I render nothing back at all?
Not so; not cold,—but very poor instead.
Ask God who knows. For frequent tears have run
The colours from my life, and left so dead
And pale a stuff, it were not fitly done
To give the same as pillow to thy head.
Go farther! let it serve to trample on.

IX

Can it be right to give what I can give?
To let thee sit beneath the fall of tears
As salt as mine, and hear the sighing years
Re-sighing on my lips renunciative
Through those infrequent smiles which fail to live
For all thy adjurations? O my fears,
That this can scarce be right! We are not peers,
So to be lovers; and I own, and grieve,
That givers of such gifts as mine are, must
Be counted with the ungenerous. Out, alas!
I will not soil thy purple with my dust,
Nor breathe my poison on thy Venice-glass,
Nor give thee any love—which were unjust.
Beloved, I only love thee! let it pass.

X

Yet, love, mere love, is beautiful indeed
And worthy of acceptation. Fire is bright,
Let temple burn, or flax. An equal light
Leaps in the flame from cedar-plank or weed.
And love is fire. And when I say at need
I love thee . . . mark! . . . _I love thee_—in thy sight
I stand transfigured, glorified aright,
With conscience of the new rays that proceed
Out of my face toward thine. There's nothing low
In love, when love the lowest: meanest creatures
Who love God, God accepts while loving so.
And what I _feel_, across the inferior features
Of what I _am_, doth flash itself, and show
How that great work of Love enhances Nature's.

XI

And therefore if to love can be desert,
I am not all unworthy. Cheeks as pale
As these you see, and trembling knees that fail
To bear the burden of a heavy heart.—
This weary minstrel-life that once was girt
To climb Aornus, and can scarce avail
To pipe now 'gainst the valley nightingale
A melancholy music,—why advert
To these things? O Belovèd, it is plain
I am not of thy worth nor for thy place!
And yet, because I love thee, I obtain
From that same love this vindicating grace,
To live on still in love, and yet in vain, . . .
To bless thee, yet renounce thee to thy face.

XII

Indeed this very love which is my boast,
And which, when rising up from breast to brow,
Doth crown me with a ruby large enow
To draw men's eyes and prove the inner cost, . . .
This love even, all my worth, to the uttermost,
I should not love withal, unless that thou
Hadst set me an example, shown me how,
When first thine earnest eyes with mine were crossed
And love called love. And thus, I cannot speak
Of love even, as a good thing of my own.
Thy soul hath snatched up mine all faint and weak
And placed it by thee on a golden throne,—
And that I love (O soul, we must be meek!)
Is by thee only, whom I love alone.

XIII

And wilt thou have me fashion into speech
The love I bear thee, finding words enough,
And hold the torch out, while the winds are rough
Between our faces, to cast light on each?—
I drop it at thy feet. I cannot teach
My hand to hold my spirit so far off
From myself . . . me . . . that I should bring thee proof
In words, of love hid in me out of reach.
Nay, let the silence of my womanhood
Commend my woman-love to thy belief,—
Seeing that I stand unwon, however wooed,
And rend the garment of my life, in brief,
By a most dauntless, voiceless fortitude,
Lest one touch of this heart convey its grief.

XIV

If thou must love me, let it be for nought
Except for love's sake only. Do not say
'I love her for her smile . . . her look . . . her way
Of speaking gently, . . . for a trick of thought
That falls in well with mine, and certes brought
A sense of pleasant ease on such a day'—
For these things in themselves, Belovèd, may
Be changed, or change for thee,—and love, so wrought
May be unwrought so. Neither love me for
Thine own dear pity's wiping my cheeks dry,—
A creature might forget to weep, who bore
Thy comfort long, and lose thy love thereby!
But love me for love's sake, that evermore
Thou may'st love on, through love's eternity.

XV

Accuse me not, beseech thee, that I wear
Too calm and sad a face in front of thine;
For we two look two ways, and cannot shine
With the same sunlight on our brow and hair.
On me thou lookest with no doubting care,
As on a bee shut in a crystalline,—
Since sorrow hath shut me safe in love's divine,
And to spread wing and fly in the outer air
Were most impossible failure, if I strove
To fail so. But I look on thee—on thee—
Beholding, besides love, the end of love,
Hearing oblivion beyond memory!
As one who sits and gazes from above,
Over the rivers to the bitter sea.

XVI

And yet, because thou overcomest so,
Because thou art more noble and like a king,
Thou canst prevail against my fears and fling
Thy purple round me, till my heart shall grow
Too close against thine heart henceforth to know
How it shook when alone. Why, conquering
May prove as lordly and complete a thing
In lifting upward, as in crushing low!
And as a vanquished soldier yields his sword
To one who lifts him from the bloody earth,—
Even so, Belovëd, I at last record,
Here ends my strife. If *thou* invite me forth,
I rise above abasement at the word.
Make thy love larger to enlarge my worth.

XVII

My poet, thou canst touch on all the notes
God set between His After and Before,
And strike up and strike off the general roar
Of the rushing worlds a melody that floats
In a serene air purely. Antidotes
Of medicated music, answering for
Mankind's forlornest uses, thou canst pour
From thence into their ears. God's will devotes
Thine to such ends, and mine to wait on thine.
How, Dearest, wilt thou have me for most use?
A hope, to sing by gladly? . . . or a fine
Sad memory, with thy songs to interfuse?
A shade, in which to sing . . . of palm or pine?
A grave, on which to rest from singing? . . . Choose.

XVIII

I never gave a lock of hair away
To a man, Dearest, except this to thee,
Which now upon my fingers thoughtfully
I ring out to the full brown length and say
'Take it.' My day of youth went yesterday;
My hair no longer bounds to my foot's glee,
Nor plant I it from rose- or myrtle-tree,
As girls do, any more. It only may
Now shade on two pale cheeks the mark of tears,
Taught drooping from the head that hangs aside
Through sorrow's trick. I thought the funeral-shears
Would take this first, but Love is justified,—
Take it thou, . . . finding pure, from all those years,
The kiss my mother left here when she died.

XIX

The soul's Rialto hath its merchandize;
I barter curl for curl upon that mart,
And from my poet's forehead to my heart
Receive this lock which outweighs argosies,—
As purply black, as erst to Pindar's eyes
The dim purpureal tresses gloomed athwart
The nine white Muse-brows. For this counterpart, . . .
The bay-crown's shade, Belovèd, I surmise,
Still lingers on thy curl, it is so black!
Thus, with a fillet of smooth-kissing breath,
I tie the shadows safe from gliding back,
And lay the gift where nothing hindereth,
Here on my heart, as on thy brow, to lack
No natural heat till mine grows cold in death.

XX

Belovèd, my Belovèd, when I think
That thou wast in the world a year ago,
What time I sat alone here in the snow
And saw no footprint, heard the silence sink
No moment at thy voice, . . . but, link by link,
Went counting all my chains as if that so
They never could fall off at any blow
Struck by thy possible hand . . . why, thus I drink
Of life's great cup of wonder! Wonderful,
Never to feel thee thrill the day or night
With personal act or speech,—nor even cull
Some prescience of thee with the blossoms white
Thou sawest growing! Atheists are as dull,
Who cannot guess God's presence out of sight.

XXI

Say over again, and yet once over again,
That thou dost love me. Though the word repeated
Should seem 'a cuckoo-song,' as thou dost treat it.
Remember, never to the hill or plain,
Valley and wood, without her cuckoo-strain
Comes the fresh Spring in all her green completed.
Belovèd, I, amid the darkness greeted
By a doubtful spirit-voice, in that doubt's pain
Cry, . . . 'Speak once more . . . thou lovest!' Who can fear
Too many stars, though each in heaven shall roll,—
Too many flowers, though each shall crown the year?
Say thou dost love me, love me, love me—toll
The silver iterance!—only minding, Dear,
To love me also in silence with thy soul.

XXII

When our two souls stand up erect and strong,
Face to face, silent, drawing nigh and nigher,
Until the lengthening wings break into fire
At either curvèd point,—what bitter wrong
Can the earth do to us, that we should not long
Be here contented? Think. In mounting higher,
The angels would press on us and aspire
To drop some golden orb of perfect song
Into our deep, dear silence. Let us stay
Rather on earth, Belovèd,—where the unfit
Contrarious moods of men recoil away
And isolate pure spirits, and permit
A place to stand and love in for a day,
With darkness and the death-hour rounding it.

XXIII

Is it indeed so? If I lay here dead,
Wouldst thou miss any life in losing mine?
And would the sun for thee more coldly shine
Because of grave-damps falling round my head?
I marvelled, my Belovèd, when I read
Thy thought so in the letter. I am thine—
But . . . *so* much to thee? Can I pour thy wine
While my hands tremble? Then my soul, instead
Of dreams of death, resumes life's lower range.
Then, love me, Love! look on me . . . breathe on me!
As brighter ladies do not count it strange,
For love, to give up acres and degree,
I yield the grave for thy sake, and exchange
My near sweet view of heaven, for earth with thee!

XXIV

Let the world's sharpness like a clasping knife
Shut in upon itself and do no harm
In this close hand of Love, now soft and warm,
And let us hear no sound of human strife
After the click of the shutting. Life to life—
I lean upon thee, Dear, without alarm,
And feel as safe as guarded by a charm
Against the stab of worldlings, who if rife
Are weak to injure. Very whitely still
The lilies of our lives may reassure
Their blossoms from their roots, accessible
Alone to heavenly dews that drop not fewer:
Growing straight, out of man's reach, on the hill.
God only, who made us rich, can make us poor.

XXV

A heavy heart, Belovèd, have I borne
From year to year until I saw thy face,
And sorrow after sorrow took the place
Of all those natural joys as lightly worn
As the stringed pearls, . . . each lifted in its turn
By a beating heart at dance-time. Hopes apace
Were changed to long despairs, till God's own grace
Could scarcely lift above the world forlorn
My heavy heart. Then *thou* didst bid me bring
And let it drop adown thy calmly great
Deep being! Fast it sinketh, as a thing
Which its own nature does precipitate,
While thine doth close above it, mediating
Betwixt the stars and the unaccomplished fate.

XXVI

I lived with visions for my company
Instead of men and women, years ago,
And found them gentle mates, nor thought to know
A sweeter music than they played to me.
But soon their trailing purple was not free
Of this world's dust,—their lutes did silent grow,
And I myself grew faint and blind below
Their vanishings eyes. Then THOU didst come . . . to be,
Belovèd, what they seemed. Their shining fronts,
Their songs, their splendours, (better, yet the same,
As river-water hallowed into fonts)
Met in thee, and from out thee overcame
My soul with satisfaction of all wants—
Because God's gifts put man's best dreams to shame.

XXVII

My own Belovèd, who hast lifted me
From this drear flat of earth where I was thrown,
And, in betwixt the languid ringlets, blown
A life-breath, till the forehead hopefully
Shines out again, as all the angels see,
Before thy saving kiss! My own, my own,
Who camest to me when the world was gone,
And I who looked for only God, found *thee!*
I find thee; I am safe, and strong, and glad.
As one who stands in dewless asphodel,
Looks backward on the tedious time he had
In the upper life,—so I, with bosom-swell,
Make witness, here, between the good and bad,
That Love, as strong as death, retrieves as well.

XXVIII

My letters! all dead paper, . . . mute and white!
And yet they seem alive and quivering
Against my tremulous hands which loose the string
And let them drop down on my knee to-night.
This said, . . . he wished to have me in his sight
Once, as a friend: this fixed a day in spring
To come and touch my hand . . . a simple thing,
Yet I wept for it!—this, . . . the paper's light . . .
Said, *Dear I love thee;* and I sank and quailed
As if God's future thundered on my past.
This said, *I am thine*—and so its ink has paled
With lying at my heart that beat too fast.
And this . . . O Love, thy words have ill availed
If, what this said, I dared repeat at last!

XXIX

I think of thee!—my thoughts do twine and bud
About thee, as wild vines, about a tree,
Put out broad leaves, and soon there's nought to see
Except the straggling green which hides the wood.
Yet, O my palm-tree, be it understood
I will not have my thoughts instead of thee
Who art dearer, better! Rather, instantly
Renew thy presence. As a strong tree should,
Rustle thy boughs and set thy trunk all bare,
And let these bands of greenery which insphere thee,
Drop heavily down, . . . burst, shattered, everywhere!
Because, in this deep joy to see and hear thee
And breathe within thy shadow a new air,
I do not think of thee—I am too near thee.

XXX

I see thine image through my tears to-night,
And yet to-day I saw thee smiling. How
Refer the cause?—Belovèd, is it thou
Or I, who makes me sad? The acolyte
Amid the chanted joy and thankful rite
May so fall flat, with pale insensate brow,
On the altar-stair. I hear thy voice and vow,
Perplexed, uncertain, since thou art out of sight,
As he, in his swooning ears, the choir's amen.
Belovèd, dost thou love? or did I see all
The glory as I dreamed, and fainted when
Too vehement light dilated my ideal,
For my soul's eyes? Will that light come again,
As now these tears come . . . falling hot and real?

XXXI

Thou comest! all is said without a word.
I sit beneath thy looks, as children do
In the noon-sun, with souls that tremble through
Their happy eyelids from an unaverred
Yet prodigal inward joy. Behold, I erred
In that last doubt! and yet I cannot rue
The sin most, but the occasion . . . that we two
Should for a moment stand unministered
By a mutal presence. Ah, keep near and close,
Thou dove-like help! and, when my fears would rise,
With thy broad heart serenely interpose.
Brood down with thy divine sufficiencies
These thoughts which tremble when bereft of those,
Like callow birds left desert to the skies.

XXXII

The first time that the sun rose on thine oath
To love me, I looked forward to the moon
To slacken all those bonds which seemed too soon
And quickly tied to make a lasting troth.
Quick-loving hearts, I thought, may quickly loathe;
And, looking on myself, I seemed not one
For such man's love!—more like an out-of-tune
Worn viol, a good singer would be wroth
To spoil his song with, and which, snatched in haste,
Is laid down at the first ill-sounding note.
I did not wrong myself so, but I placed
A wrong on *thee*. For perfect strains may float
'Neath master-hands, from instruments defaced,—
And great souls, at one stroke, may do and dote.

XXXIII

Yes, call me by my pet-name! let me hear
The name I used to run at, when a child,
From innocent play, and leave the cowslips piled,
To glance up in some face that proved me dear
With the look of its eyes. I miss the clear
Fond voices which, being drawn and reconciled
Into the music of Heaven's undefiled,
Call me no longer. Silence on the bier,
While I call God . . . call God!—So let thy mouth
Be heir to those who are now exanimate.
Gather the north flowers to complete the south,
And catch the early love up in the late.
Yes, call me by that name,—and I, in truth,
With the same heart, will answer and not wait.

XXXIV

With the same heart, I said, I'll answer thee
As those, when thou shalt call me by my name—
Lo, the vain promise! is the same, the same,
Perplexed and ruffled by life's strategy?
When called before, I told how hastily
I dropped my flowers or brake off from a game,
To run and answer with the smile that came
At play last moment, and went on with me
Through my obedience. When I answer now,
I drop a grave thought, break from solitude;
Yet still my heart goes to thee . . . ponder how . . .
Not as to a single good, but all my good!
Lay thy hand on it, best one, and allow
That no child's foot could run fast as this blood.

XXXV

If I leave all for thee, wilt thou exchange
And be all to me? Shall I never miss
Home-talk and blessing and the common kiss
That comes to each in turn, nor count it strange,
When I look up, to drop on a new range
Of walls and floors, . . . another home than this?
Nay, wilt thou fill that place by me which is
Filled by dead eyes too tender to know change?
That's hardest. If to conquer love, has tried,
To conquer grief, tries more . . . as all things prove,
For grief indeed is love and grief beside.
Alas, I have grieved so I am hard to love.
Yet love me—wilt thou? Open thine heart wide,
And fold within, the wet wings of thy dove.

XXXVI

When we met first and loved, I did not build
Upon the event with marble. Could it mean
To last, a love set pendulous between
Sorrow and sorrow? Nay, I rather thrilled,
Distrusting every light that seemed to gild
The onward path, and feared to overlean
A finger even. And, though I have grown serene
And strong since then, I think that God has willed
A still renewable fear . . . O love, O troth . . .
Lest these enclaspèd hands should never hold,
This mutual kiss drop down between us both
As an unowned thing, once the lips being cold.
And Love, be false! if *he*, to keep one oath,
Must lose one joy, by his life's star foretold.

XXXVII

Pardon, oh, pardon, that my soul should make
Of all that strong divineness which I know
For thine and thee, an image only so
Formed of the sand, and fit to shift and break.
It is that distant years which did not take
Thy sovranty, recoiling with a blow,
Have forced my swimming brain to undergo
Their doubt and dread, and blindly to forsake
Thy purity of likeness and distort
Thy worthiest love to a worthless counterfeit.
As if a shipwrecked Pagan, safe in port,
His guardian sea-god to commemorate,
Should set a sculptured porpoise, gills a-snort
And vibrant tail, within the temple-gate.

XXXVIII

First time he kissed me, he but only kissed
The fingers of this hand wherewith I write;
And ever since, it grew more clean and white, . . .
Slow to world-greetings, quick with its 'Oh, list,'
When the angels speak. A ring of amethyst
I could not wear here, plainer to my sight,
Than that first kiss. The second passed in height
The first, and sought the forehead, and half missed,
Half falling on the hair. O beyond meed!
That was the chrism of love, which love's own crown
With sanctifying sweetness, did precede.
The third upon my lips was folded down
In perfect, purple state; since when, indeed,
I have been proud and said, 'My love, my own.'

XXXIX

Because thou hast the power and own'st the grace
To look through and behind this mask of me,
(Against which, years have beat thus blanchingly
With their rains,) and behold my soul's true face,
The dim and weary witness of life's race!—
Because thou hast the faith and love to see,
Through that same soul's distracting lethargy,
The patient angel waiting for a place
In the new heavens!—because nor sin nor woe,
Nor God's infliction, nor death's neighbourhood,
Nor all which others viewing, turn to go, . . .
Nor all which makes me tired of all, self-viewed, . . .
Nothing repels thee, . . . Dearest, teach me so
To pour out gratitude, as thou dost, good.

XL

Oh, yes! they love through all this world of ours!
I will not gainsay love, called love forsooth.
I have heard love talked in my early youth,
And since, not so long back but that the flowers
Then gathered, smell still. Mussulmans and Giaours
Throw kerchiefs at a smile, and have no ruth
For any weeping. Polypheme's white tooth
Slips on the nut if, after frequent showers,
The shell is over-smooth,—and not so much
Will turn the thing called love, aside to hate
Or else to oblivion. But thou art not such
A lover, my Belovèd! thou canst wait
Through sorrow and sickness, to bring souls to touch
And think it soon when others cry 'Too late.'

XLI

I thank all who have loved me in their hearts,
With thanks and love from mine. Deep thanks to all
Who paused a little near the prison-wall
To hear my music in its louder parts
Ere they went onward, each one to the mart's
Or temple's occupation, beyond call.
But thou, who, in my voice's sink and fall
When the sob took it, thy divinest Art's
Own instrument didst drop down at thy foot
To harken what I said between my tears, . . .
Instruct me how to thank thee!—Oh, to shoot
My soul's full meaning into future years,
That *they* should lend it utterance, and salute
Love that endures, from Life that disappears!

XLII

'My future will not copy fair my past'—
I wrote that once; and thinking at my side
My ministering life-angel justified
The word by his appealing look upcast
To the white throne of God, I turned at last,
And there, instead, saw thee, not unallied
To angels in thy soul! Then I, long tried
By natural ills, received the comfort fast,
While budding, at thy sight, my pilgrim's staff
Gave out green leaves with morning dews impearled.
I seek no copy now of life's first half:
Leave here the pages with long musing curled,
And write me new my future's epigraph,
New angel mine, unhoped for in the world!

XLIII

How do I love thee? Let me count the ways.
I love thee to the depth and breadth and height
My soul can reach, when feeling out of sight
For the ends of Being and ideal Grace.
I love thee to the level of everyday's
Most quiet need, by sun and candlelight.
I love thee freely, as men strive for Right;
I love thee purely, as they turn from Praise.
I love thee with the passion put to use
In my old griefs, and with my childhood's faith.
I love thee with a love I seemed to lose
With my lost saints,—I love thee with the breath,
Smiles, tears, of all my life!—and, if God choose,
I shall but love thee better after death.

XLIV

Belovèd, thou hast brought me many flowers
Plucked in the garden, all the summer through
And winter, and it seemed as if they grew
In this close room, nor missed the sun and showers.
So, in the like name of that love of ours,
Take back these thoughts which here unfolded too,
And which on warm and cold days I withdrew
From my heart's ground. Indeed, those beds and bowers
Be overgrown with bitter weeds and rue,
And wait thy weeding; yet here's eglantine,
Here's ivy!—take them, as I used to do
Thy flowers, and keep them where they shall not pine.
Instruct thine eyes to keep their colours true,
And tell thy soul, their roots are left in mine.

CASA GUIDI WINDOWS
PART ONE
(1851)

Preface

The Casa Guidi in Florence was the only real home the Brownings ever had (they rented it, with one short break, from 1847 to 1861 although much of that time they were away and sub-let it). Their first-floor apartment looked onto the side of the San Felice church and from a narrow balcony the Brownings could see what was happening in the street below.

On 12th September 1847, her first weddding anniversary, Elizabeth Barrett Browning watched a magnificent procession celebrating the granting of certain civil liberties to the Florentines by their Grand Duke. She was inspired to write a poem in praise of Italian liberalism. It was finished in the spring of 1848 and entitled "Meditation in Tuscany". The editor of *Blackwood's* magazine, to whom it was sent, declined to publish it, claiming it was already out of date (he was right —Italian liberalism had proved a mirage at that stage). He also doubted if English readers would be interested in the subject. Elizabeth took the rejection well and resolved to write another poem expressing her disappointment that Italian freedom from Austrian oppression was still an illusion. When she finished it she put the two poems together and called the whole *Casa Guidi Windows*.

Part One (originally "Meditation in Tuscany") is by far the most successful of the two parts. It has a vigour and pace, which is lacking in the second. She is proud to introduce herself as the self-appointed poet of the Italian Risorgimento (although she did sound a note of caution about the future of the liberal movement which her critics did not pick up). *Casa Guidi Windows* was an ambitious project which she feared, correctly, would be misunderstood. It received little critical attention and sold badly.

CASA GUIDI WINDOWS
PART ONE

I heard last night a little child go singing
   'Neath Casa Guidi windows, by the church,
O bella libertà, O bella! stringing
   The same words still on notes he went in search
So high for, you concluded the upspringing
   Of such a nimble bird to sky from perch
Must leave the whole bush in a tremble green,
   And that the heart of Italy must beat,
While such a voice had leave to rise serene
   'Twixt church and palace of a Florence street!
A little child, too, who not long had been
   By mother's finger steadied on his feet,
And still *O bella libertà* he sang.

Then I thought, musing, of the innumerous
   Sweet songs which still for Italy outrang
From older singers' lips, who sang not thus
   Exultingly and purely, yet, with pang
Fast sheathed in music, touched the heart of us
   So finely, that the pity scarcely pained.
I thought how Filicaja led on others,
   Bewailers for their Italy enchained,
And how they called her childless among mothers,
   Widow of empires, aye, and scarce refrained
Cursing her beauty to her face, as brothers
   Might a shamed sister's,—'Had she been less fair
She were less wretched,'—how, evoking so
   From congregated wrong and heaped despair
Of men and women writhing under blow,
   Harrowed and hideous in a filthy lair,
Some personating Image, wherein woe
   Was wrapt in beauty from offending much,
They called it Cybele, or Niobe,

[241]

Or laid it corpse-like on a bier for such,
Where all the world might drop for Italy
    Those cadenced tears which burn not where they touch,—
'Juliet of nations, canst thou die as we?
    And was the violet crown that crowned thy head
So over-large, though new buds made it rough,
    It slipped down and across thine eyelids dead,
O sweet, fair Juliet?' Of such songs enough,
    Too many of such complaints! behold, instead,
Void at Verona, Juliet's marble trough.
    As void as that is, are all images
Men set between themselves and actual wrong,
    To catch the weight of pity, meet the stress
Of conscience,—since 'tis easier to gaze long
    On mournful masks, and sad effigies,
Than on real, live, weak creatures crushed by strong.

    For me who stand in Italy to-day,
Where worthier poets stood and sang before,
    I kiss their footsteps, yet their words gainsay.
I can but muse in hope upon this shore
    Of golden Arno as it shoots away
Through Florence' heart beneath her bridges four!
    Bent bridges, seeming to strain off like bows,
And tremble while the arrowy undertide
    Shoots on and cleaves the marble as it goes,
And strikes up palace-walls on either side,
    And froths the cornice out in glittering rows,
With doors and windows quaintly multiplied,
    And terrace-sweeps, and gazers upon all,
By whom if flower or kerchief were thrown out
    From any lattice there, the same would fall
Into the river underneath no doubt,
    It runs so close and fast 'twixt wall and wall.
How beautiful! the mountains from without
    In silence listen for the word said next.

What word will men say,—here where Giotto planted
   His campanile, like an unperplexed
Fine question Heaven-ward, touching the things granted
   A noble people who, being greatly vexed
In act, in aspiration keep undaunted?
   What word will God say? Michel's Night and Day
And Dawn and Twilight wait in marble scorn,
   Like dogs upon a dunghill, couched on clay
From whence the Medicean stamp's outworn,
   The final putting off of all such sway
By all such hands, and freeing of the unborn
   In Florence and the great world outside Florence.
Three hundred years his patient statues wait
   In that small chapel of the dim St. Lawrence.
Day's eyes are breaking bold and passionate
   Over his shoulder, and will flash abhorrence
On darkness and with level looks meet fate,
   When once loose from that marble film of theirs;
The Night has wild dreams in her sleep, the Dawn
   Is haggard as the sleepless, Twilight wears
A sort of horror; as the veil withdrawn
   'Twixt the artist's soul and works had left them heirs
Of speechless thoughts which would not quail nor fawn,
   Of angers and contempts, of hope and love;
For not without a meaning did he place
   The princely Urbino on the seat above
With everlasting shadow on his face,
   While the slow dawns and twilights disapprove
The ashes of his long-extinguished race,
   Which never more shall clog the feet of men.
I do believe, divinest Angelo,
   That winter-hour, in Via Larga, when
They bade thee build a statue up in snow,
   And straight that marvel of thine art again
Dissolved beneath the sun's Italian glow,
   Thine eyes, dilated with the plastic passion,

Thawing too, in drops of wounded manhood, since,
    To mock alike thine art and indignation,
Laughed at the palace-window the new prince,—
    ('Aha! this genius needs for exaltation,
When all's said, and howe'er the proud may wince,
    A little marble from our princely mines!')
I do believe that hour thou laughedst too,
    For the whole sad world and for thy Florentines,
After those few tears—which were only few!
    That as, beneath the sun, the grand white lines
Of thy snow-statue trembled and withdrew,—
    The head, erect as Jove's, being palsied first,
The eyelids flattened, the full brow turned blank,—
    The right hand, raised but now as if it cursed,
Dropt, a mere snowball, (till the people sank
    Their voices, though a louder laughter burst
From the royal window) thou couldst proudly thank
    God and the prince for promise and presage,
And laugh the laugh back, I think verily,
    Thine eyes being purged by tears of righteous rage
To read a wrong into a prophecy,
    And measure a true great man's heritage
Against a mere great duke's posterity.
    I think thy soul said then, 'I do not need
A princedom and its quarries, after all;
    For if I write, paint, carve a word, indeed,
On book or board or dust, on floor or wall,
    The same is kept of God, who taketh heed
That not a letter of the meaning fall
    Or ere it touch and teach His world's deep heart,
Outlasting, therefore, all your lordships, sir!
    So keep your stone, beseech you, for your part,
To cover up your grave-place and refer
    The proper titles; _I_ live by my art.
The thought I threw into this snow shall stir
    This gazing people when their gaze is done;

And the tradition of your act and mine,
    When all the snow is melted in the sun,
Shall gather up, for unborn men, a sign
    Of what is the true princedom,—aye, and none
Shall laugh that day, except the drunk with wine.'

    Amen, great Angelo! the day's at hand.
If many laugh not on it, shall we weep?
    Much more we must not, let us understand.
Through rhymers sonneteering in their sleep,
    And archaists mumbling dry bones up the land,
And sketchers lauding ruined towns a-heap,—
    Through all that drowsy hum of voices smooth,
The hopeful bird mounts carolling from brake,
    The hopeful child, with leaps to catch his growth,
Sings open-eyed for liberty's sweet sake!
    And I, a singer also, from my youth,
Prefer to sing with these who are awake,
    With birds, with babes, with men who will not fear
The baptism of the holy morning dew,
    (And many of such wakers now are here,
Complete in their anointed manhood, who
    Will greatly dare and greatlier persevere,)
Than join those old thin voices with my new,
    And sigh for Italy with some safe sigh
Cooped up in music 'twixt an oh and ah,—
    Nay, hand in hand with that young child, will I
Go singing rather, *'Bella libertà,'*
    Than, with those poets, croon the dead or cry
'Se tu men bella fossi, Italia!'

    'Less wretched if less fair.' Perhaps a truth
Is so far plain in this—that Italy,
    Long trammelled with the purple of her youth
Against her age's ripe activity,
    Sits still upon her tombs, without death's ruth,

But also without life's brave energy.
   'Now tell us what is Italy?' men ask:
And others answer, 'Virgil, Cicero,
   Catullus, Cæsar.' What beside? to task
The memory closer—'Why, Boccaccio,
   Dante, Petrarca,'—and if still the flask
Appears to yield its wine by drops too slow,—
   'Angelo, Raffael, Pergolese,'—all
Whose strong hearts beat through stone, or charged again
   The paints with fire of souls electrical,
Or broke up heaven for music. What more then?
   Why, then, no more. The chaplet's last beads fall
In naming the last saintship within ken,
   And, after that, none prayeth in the land.
Alas, this Italy has too long swept
   Heroic ashes up for hour-glass sand;
Of her own past, impassioned nympholept!
   Consenting to be nailed here by the hand
To the very bay-tree under which she stepped
   A queen of old, and plucked a leafy branch.
And, licensing the world too long indeed
   To use her broad phylacteries to staunch
And stop her bloody lips, she takes no heed
   How one clear word would draw an avalanche
Of living sons around her, to succeed
   The vanished generations. Can she count
These oil-eaters, with large, live, mobile mouths
   Agape for maccaroni, in the amount
Of consecrated heroes of her south's
   Bright rosary? The pitcher at the fount,
The gift of gods, being broken, she much loathes
   To let the ground-leaves of the place confer
A natural bowl. So henceforth she would seem
   No nation, but the poet's pensioner,
With alms from every land of song and dream,
   While aye her pipers sadly pipe of her,

Until their proper breaths, in that extreme
    Of sighing, split the reed on which they played!
Of which, no more. But never say 'no more'
    To Italy's life! Her memories undismayed
Still argue 'evermore,'—her graves implore
    Her future to be strong and not afraid;
Her very statues send their looks before.

    We do not serve the dead—the past is past!
God lives, and lifts his glorious mornings up
    Before the eyes of men, awake at last,
Who put away the meats they used to sup,
    And down upon the dust of earth outcast
The dregs remaining of the ancient cup,
    Then turn to wakeful prayer and worthy act.
The dead, upon their awful 'vantage ground,
    The sun not in their faces,—shall abstract
No more our strength: we will not be discrowned
    As guardians of their crowns; nor deign transact
A barter of the present, for a sound
    Of good, so counted in the foregone days.
O Dead, ye shall no longer cling to us
    With rigid hands of desiccating praise,
And drag us backward by the garment thus,
    To stand and laud you in long-drawn virelays!
We will not henceforth be oblivious
    Of our own lives, because ye lived before,
Nor of our acts, because ye acted well.
    We thank you that ye first unlatched the door,
But will not make it inaccessible
    By thankings on the threshold any more.
We hurry onward to extinguish hell
    With our fresh souls, our younger hope, and God's
Maturity of purpose. Soon shall we
    Die also! and, that then our periods
Of life may round themselves to memory,

As smoothly as on our graves the burial-sods,
We now must look to it to excel as ye,
    And bear our age as far, unlimited
By the last mind-mark! so, to be invoked
    By future generations, as their Dead.

'Tis true that when the dust of death has choked
    A great man's voice, the common words he said
Turn oracles,—the common thoughts he yoked
    Like horses, draw like griffins!—this is true
And acceptable. I, too, should desire,
    When men make record, with the flowers they strew,
'Savonarola's soul went out in fire
    Upon our Grand-duke's piazza, and burned through
A moment first, or ere he did expire,
    The veil betwixt the right and wrong, and showed
How near God sate and judged the judges there,—'
    Upon the self-same pavement overstrewed,
To cast my violets with as reverent care,
    And prove that all the winters which have snowed
Cannot snow out the scent from stones and air,
    Of a sincere man's virtues. This was he,
Savonarola, who, while Peter sank
    With his whole boat-load, called courageously
'Wake Christ, wake Christ!'—Who, having tried the tank
    Of old church-waters used for baptistry
Ere Luther came to spill them, swore they stank!
    Who also by a princely deathbed cried,
'Loose Florence, or God will not loose thy soul!'
    Then fell back the Magnificent and died
Beneath the star-look, shooting from the cowl,
    Which turned to wormwood bitterness the wide
Deep sea of his ambitions. It were foul
    To grudge Savonarola and the rest
Their violets! rather pay them quick and fresh!
    The emphasis of death makes manifest

The eloquence of action in our flesh;
　And men who, living, were but dimly guessed,
When once free from their life's entangled mesh,
　Show their full length in graves, or oft indeed
Exaggerate their stature, in the flat,
　To noble admirations which exceed
Most nobly, yet will calculate in that
　But accurately. We, who are the seed
Of buried creatures, if we turned and spat
　Upon our antecedents, we were vile.
Bring violets rather! If these had not walked
　Their furlong, could we hope to walk our mile?
Therefore bring violets. Yet if we, self-baulked,
　Stand still, a-strewing violets all the while,
These moved in vain, of whom we have vainly talked.
　So rise up henceforth with a cheerful smile,
And having strewn the violets, reap the corn,
　And having reaped and garnered, bring the plough
And draw new furrows 'neath the healthy morn,
　And plant the great Hereafter in this Now.

Of old 'twas so. How step by step was worn,
　As each man gained on each, securely!—how
Each by his own strength sought his own ideal,—
　The ultimate Perfection leaning bright
From out the sun and stars, to bless the leal
　And earnest search of all for Fair and Right,
Through doubtful forms, by earth accounted real!
　Because old Jubal blew into delight
The souls of men, with clear-piped melodies,
　If youthful Asaph were content at most
To draw from Jubal's grave, with listening eyes,
　Traditionary music's floating ghost
Into the grass-grown silence, were it wise?
　And was't not wiser, Jubal's breath being lost,
That Miriam clashed her cymbals to surprise

The sun between her white arms flung apart,
With new, glad, golden sounds? that David's strings
  O'erflowed his hand with music from his heart?
So harmony grows full from many springs,
  And happy accident turns holy art.

You enter, in your Florence wanderings,
  The church of St. Maria Novella. Pass
The left stair, where at plague-time Macchiavel
  Saw One with set fair face as in a glass,
Dressed out against the fear of death and hell,
  Rustling her silks in pauses of the mass,
To keep the thought off how her husband fell,
  When she left home, stark dead across her feet,—
The stair leads up to what the Orgagnas save
  Of Dante's dæmons; you, in passing it,
Ascend the right stair from the farther nave,
  To muse in a small chapel scarcely lit
By Cimabue's Virgin. Bright and brave,
  That picture was accounted, mark, of old.
A king stood bare before its sovran grace,
  A reverent people shouted to behold
The picture, not the king, and even the place
  Containing such a miracle, grew bold,
Named the Glad Borgo from that beauteous face,—
  Which thrilled the artist, after work, to think
His own ideal Mary-smile should stand
  So very near him,—he, within the brink
Of all that glory, let in by his hand
  With too divine a rashness! Yet none shrink
Who come to gaze here now—albeit 'twas planned
  Sublimely in the thought's simplicity.
The Lady, throned in empyreal state,
  Minds only the young babe upon her knee,
While sidelong angels bear the royal weight,
  Prostrated meekly, smiling tenderly

Oblivion of their wings; the Child thereat
    Stretching its hand like God. If any should,
Because of some stiff draperies and loose joints,
    Gaze scorn down from the heights of Raffaelhood,
On Cimabue's picture,—Heaven anoints
    The head of no such critic, and his blood
The poet's curse strikes full on and appoints
    To ague and cold spasms for evermore.
A noble picture! worthy of the shout
    Wherewith along the streets the people bore
Its cherub faces, which the sun threw out
    Until they stooped and entered the church door!—
Yet rightly was young Giotto talked about,
    Whom Cimabue found among the sheep,
And knew, as gods know gods, and carried home
    To paint the things he had painted, with a deep
And fuller insight, and so overcome
    His chapel-lady with a heavenlier sweep
Of light. For thus we mount into the sum
    Of great things known or acted. I hold, too,
That Cimabue smiled upon the lad,
    At the first stroke which passed what he could do,—
Or else his Virgin's smile had never had
    Such sweetness in 't. All great men who foreknew
Their heirs in art, for art's sake have been glad,
    And bent their old white heads as if uncrowned,
Fanatics of their pure ideals still
    Far more than of their triumphs, which were found
With some less vehement struggle of the will.
    If old Margheritone trembled, swooned,
And died despairing at the open sill
    Of other men's achievements, (who achieved,
By loving art beyond the master!) he
    Was old Margheritone, and conceived
Never, at first youth and most ecstasy,
    A Virgin like that dream of one, which heaved

The death-sigh from his heart. If wistfully
  Margheritone sickened at the smell
Of Cimabue's laurel, let him go!—
  For Cimabue stood up very well
In spite of Giotto's—and Angelico,
  The artist-saint, kept smiling in his cell
The smile with which he welcomed the sweet slow
  Inbreak of angels, (whitening through the dim
That he might paint them!) while the sudden sense
  Of Raffael's future was revealed to him
By force of his own fair works' competence.
  The same blue waters where the dolphins swim
Suggest the tritons. Through the blue Immense,
  Strike out, all swimmers! cling not in the way
Of one another, so to sink; but learn
  The strong man's impulse, catch the fresh'ning spray
He throws up in his motions, and discern
  By his clear, westering eye, the time of day.
Thou, God, hast set us worthy gifts to earn,
  Besides thy heaven and Thee! and when I say
There's room here for the weakest man alive
  To live and die,—there's room too, I repeat,
For all the strongest to live well, and strive
  Their own way, by their individual heat,—
Like some new bee-swarm leaving the old hive,
  Despite the wax which tempts so violet-sweet.
Then let the living live, the dead retain
  Their grave-cold flowers!—though honour's best supplied,
By bringing actions, to prove theirs not vain.

Cold graves, we say? It shall be testified
That living men who burn in heart and brain,
  Without the dead were colder. If we tried
To sink the past beneath our feet, be sure
  The future would not stand. Precipitate
This old roof from the shrine—and, insecure,

The nesting swallows fly off, mate from mate.
How scant the gardens, if the graves were fewer!
  The tall green poplars grew no longer straight,
Whose tops not looked to Troy. Would any fight
  For Athens, and not swear by Marathon?
Who dared build temples, without tombs in sight?
  Or live, without some dead man's benison?
Or seek truth, hope for good, and strive for right,
  If, looking up, he saw not in the sun
Some angel of the martyrs all day long
  Standing and waiting? Your last rhythm will need
Your earliest key-note. Could I sing this song,
  If my dead masters had not taken heed
To help the heavens and earth to make me strong,
  As the wind ever will find out some reed,
And touch it to such issues as belong
  To such a frail thing? None may grudge the dead,
Libations from full cups. Unless we choose
  To look back to the hills behind us spread,
The plains before us, sadden and confuse;
  If orphaned, we are disinherited.

I would but turn these lachrymals to use,
  And pour fresh oil in from the olive grove,
To furnish them as new lamps. Shall I say
  What made my heart beat with exulting love,
A few weeks back?—

                     . . . . The day was such a day
  As Florence owes the sun. The sky above,
Its weight upon the mountains seemed to lay,
  And palpitate in glory, like a dove
Who has flown too fast, full-hearted!—take away
  The image! for the heart of man beat higher
That day in Florence, flooding all her streets
  And piazzas with a tumult and desire.
The people, with accumulated heats,

And faces turned one way, as if one fire
Both drew and flushed them, left their ancient beats,
    And went up toward the palace-Pitti wall,
To thank their Grand-duke, who, not quite of course,
    Had graciously permitted, at their call,
The citizens to use their civic force
    To guard their civic homes. So, one and all,
The Tuscan cities streamed up to the source
    Of this new good, at Florence, taking it
As good so far, presageful of more good,—
    The first torch of Italian freedom, lit
To toss in the next tiger's face who should
    Approach too near them in a greedy fit,—
The first pulse of an even flow of blood,
    To prove the level of Italian veins
Toward rights perceived and granted. How we gazed
    From Casa Guidi windows, while, in trains
Of orderly procession—banners raised,
    And intermittent burst of martial strains
Which died upon the shout, as if amazed
    By gladness beyond music—they passed on!
The Magistracy, with insignia, passed,—
    And all the people shouted in the sun,
And all the thousand windows which had cast
    A ripple of silks, in blue and scarlet, down,
(As if the houses overflowed at last,)
    Seemed growing larger with fair heads and eyes.
The Lawyers passed,—and still arose the shout,
    And hands broke from the windows to surprise
Those grave calm brows with bay-tree leaves thrown out.
    The Priesthood passed,—the friars with worldly-wise
Keen sidelong glances from their beards about
    The street to see who shouted! many a monk
Who takes a long rope in the waist, was there!
    Whereat the popular exultation drunk
With indrawn 'vivas' the whole sunny air,

While, through the murmuring windows, rose and sunk
A cloud of kerchiefed hands,—'The church makes fair
　　Her welcome in the new Pope's name.' Ensued
The black sign of the 'Martyrs!' (name no name,
　　But count the graves in silence.) Next, were viewed
The Artists; next, the Trades; and after came
　　The People,—flag and sign, and rights as good,—
And very loud the shout was for that same
　　Motto, 'Il popolo.' IL POPOLO,—
The word means dukedom, empire, majesty,
　　And kings in such an hour might read it so.
And next, with banners, each in his degree,
　　Deputed representatives a-row
Of every separate state of Tuscany.
　　Siena's she-wolf, bristling on the fold
Of the first flag, preceded Pisa's hare,
　　And Massa's lion floated calm in gold,
Pienza's following with his silver stare.
　　Arezzo's steed pranced clear from bridle-hold,—
And well might shout our Florence, greeting there
　　These, and more brethren. Last, the world had sent
The various children of her teeming flanks—
　　Greeks, English, French—as if to a parliament
Of lovers of her Italy in ranks,
　　Each bearing its land's symbol reverent.
At which the stones seemed breaking into thanks
　　And rattling up the sky, such sounds in proof
Arose; the very house-walls seemed to bend;
　　The very windows, up from door to roof,
Flashed out a rapture of bright heads, to mend
　　With passionate looks, the gesture's whirling off
A hurricane of leaves. Three hours did end
　　While all these passed; and ever in the crowd,
Rude men, unconscious of the tears that kept
　　Their beards moist, shouted; some few laughed aloud,
And none asked any why they laughed and wept.

[255]

Friends kissed each other's cheeks, and foes long vowed
More warmly did it,—two-months' babies leapt
    Right upward in their mother's arms, whose black,
Wide, glittering eyes looked elsewhere; lovers pressed
    Each before either, neither glancing back;
And peasant maidens, smoothly 'tired and tressed,
    Forgot to finger on their throats the slack
Great pearl-strings; while old blind men would not rest,
    But pattered with their staves and slid their shoes
Along the stones, and smiled as if they saw.
    O heaven, I think that day had noble use
Among God's days. So near stood Right and Law,
    Both mutually forborne! Law would not bruise,
Nor Right deny, and each in reverent awe
    Honoured the other. And if, ne'ertheless,
That good day's sun delivered to the vines
    No charta, and the liberal Duke's excess
Did scarce exceed a Guelf's or Ghibelline's
    In any special actual righteousness
Of what that day he granted, still the signs
    Are good and full of promise, we must say,
When multitudes approach their kings with prayers
    And kings concede their people's right to pray,
Both in one sunshine. Griefs are not despairs,
    So uttered, nor can royal claims dismay
When men from humble homes and ducal chairs,
    Hate wrong together. It was well to view
Those banners ruffled in a ruler's face
    Inscribed, 'Live freedom, union, and all true
Brave patriots who are aided by God's grace!'
    Nor was it ill, when Leopoldo drew
His little children to the window-place
    He stood in at the Pitti, to suggest
They too should govern as the people willed.
    What a cry rose then! some, who saw the best,
Declared his eyes filled up and overfilled

With good warm human tears which unrepressed
Ran down. I like his face; the forehead's build
　　Has no capacious genius, yet perhaps
Sufficient comprehension,—mild and sad,
　　And careful nobly,—not with care that wraps
Self-loving hearts, to stifle and make mad,
　　But careful with the care that shuns a lapse
Of faith and duty, studious not to add
　　A burden in the gathering of a gain.
And so, God save the Duke, I say with those
　　Who that day shouted it, and while dukes reign,
May all wear in the visible overflows
　　Of spirit, such a look of careful pain!
For God must love it better than repose.

And all the people who went up to let
　　Their hearts out to that Duke, as has been told—
Where guess ye that the living people met,
　　Kept tryst, formed ranks, chose leaders, first unrolled
Their banners?
　　　　　　　　　In the Loggia? where is set
　　Cellini's godlike Perseus, bronze—or gold—
(How name the metal, when the statue flings
　　Its soul so in your eyes?) with brow and sword
Superbly calm, as all opposing things,
　　Slain with the Gorgon, were no more abhorred
Since ended?
　　　　　　　　　No, the people sought no wings
　　From Perseus in the Loggia, nor implored
An inspiration in the place beside,
　　From that dim bust of Brutus, jagged and grand,
Where Buonarroti passionately tried
　　From out the close-clenched marble to demand
The head of Rome's sublimest homicide,—
　　Then dropt the quivering mallet from his hand,
Despairing he could find no model-stuff

Of Brutus, in all Florence, where he found
The gods and gladiators thick enough.
    Nor there! the people chose still holier ground!
The people, who are simple, blind, and rough,
    Know their own angels, after looking round.
Whom chose they then? where met they?

                            On the stone
    Called Dante's,—a plain flat stone, scarce discerned
From others in the pavement,—whereupon
    He used to bring his quiet chair out, turned
To Brunelleschi's church, and pour alone
    The lava of his spirit when it burned.
It is not cold to-day. O passionate
    Poor Dante, who, a banished Florentine,
Didst sit austere at banquets of the great,
    And muse upon this far-off stone of thine,
And think how oft some passer used to wait
    A moment, in the golden day's decline,
With 'Good night, dearest Dante!'—well, good night!
    I muse now, Dante, and think, verily,
Though chapelled in the byeway, out of sight,
    Ravenna's bones would thrill with ecstasy,
Could'st know thy favourite stone's elected right
    As tryst-place for thy Tuscans to foresee
Their earliest chartas from. Good night, good morn,
    Henceforward, Dante! now my soul is sure
That thine is better comforted of scorn,
    And looks down earthward in completer cure,
Than when, in Santa Croce church forlorn
    Of any corpse, the architect and hewer
Did pile the empty marbles as thy tomb.
    For now thou art no longer exiled, now
Best honoured!—we salute thee who art come
    Back to the old stone with a softer brow
Than Giotto drew upon the wall, for some

Good lovers of our age to track and plough
Their way to, through time's ordures stratified,
    And startle broad awake into the dull
Bargello chamber! now, thou'rt milder eyed,—
    Now Beatrix may leap up glad to cull
Thy first smile, even in heaven and at her side,
    Like that which, nine years old, looked beautiful
At May-game. What do I say? I only meant
    That tender Dante loved his Florence well,
While Florence, now, to love him is content;
    And, mark ye, that the piercingest sweet smell
Of love's dear incense by the living sent
    To find the dead, is not accessible
To lazy livers! no narcotic,—not
    Swung in a censer to a sleepy tune,—
But trod out in the morning air, by hot
    Quick spirits, who tread firm to ends foreshown,
And use the name of greatness unforgot,
    To meditate what greatness may be done.

For Dante sits in heaven, and ye stand here,
    And more remains for doing, all must feel,
Than trysting on his stone from year to year
    To shift processions, civic toe to heel,
The town's thanks to the Pitti. Are ye freer
    For what was felt that day? a chariot-wheel
May spin fast, yet the chariot never roll.
    But if that day suggested something good,
And bettered, with one purpose, soul by soul,—
    Better means freer. A land's brotherhood
Is most puissant: men, upon the whole,
    Are what they can be,—nations, what they would.

Will, therefore, to be strong, thou Italy!
    Will to be noble! Austrian Metternich
Can fix no yoke unless the neck agree;

And thine is like the lion's when the thick
Dews shudder from it, and no man would be
    The stroker of his mane, much less would prick
His nostril with a reed. When nations roar
    Like lions, who shall tame them, and defraud
Of the due pasture by the river-shore?
    Roar, therefore! shake your dew-laps dry abroad.
The amphitheatre with open door
    Leads back upon the benchers, who applaud
The last spear-thruster.

                              Yet the Heavens forbid
    That we should call on passion to confront
The brutal with the brutal, and, amid
    This ripening world, suggest a lion's-hunt
And lion's-vengeance for the wrongs men did
    And do now, though the spears are getting blunt.
We only call, because the sight and proof
    Of lion-strength hurts nothing; and to show
A lion-heart, and measure paw with hoof,
    Helps something, even, and will instruct a foe
As well as the onslaught, how to stand aloof!
    Or else the world gets past the mere brute blow
Or given or taken. Children use the fist
    Until they are of age to use the brain;
And so we needed Cæsars to assist
    Man's justice, and Napoleons to explain
God's counsel, when a point was nearly missed,
    Until our generations should attain
Christ's stature nearer. Not that we, alas,
    Attain already; but a single inch
Will raise to look down on the swordsman's pass,
    As knightly Roland on the coward's flinch:
And, after chloroform and ether-gas,
    We find out slowly what the bee and finch
Have ready found, through Nature's lamp in each,

How to our races we may justify
Our individual claims, and, as we reach
    Our own grapes, bend the top vines to supply
The children's uses,—how to fill a breach
    With olive branches,—how to quench a lie
With truth, and smite a foe upon the cheek
    With Christ's most conquering kiss. Why, these are things
Worth a great nation's finding, to prove weak
    The 'glorious arms' of military kings.
And so with wide embrace, my England, seek
    To stifle the bad heat and flickerings
Of this world's false and nearly expended fire!
    Draw palpitating arrows to the wood,
And twang abroad thy high hopes, and thy higher
    Resolves, from that most virtuous altitude!
Till nations shall unconsciously aspire
    By looking up to thee, and learn that good
And glory are not different. Announce law
    By freedom; exalt chivalry by peace;
Instruct how clear calm eyes can overawe,
    And how pure hands, stretched simply to release
A bond-slave, will not need a sword to draw
    To be held dreadful. O my England, crease
Thy purple with no alien agonies!
    No struggles toward encroachment, no vile war!
Disband thy captains, change thy victories,
    Be henceforth prosperous as the angels are,
Helping, not humbling.

                                Drums and battle cries
    Go out in music of the morning star—
And soon we shall have thinkers in the place
    Of fighters, each found able as a man
To strike electric influence through a race,
    Unstayed by city-wall and barbican.
The poet shall look grander in the face

Than even of old, (when he of Greece began
To sing 'that Achillean wrath which slew
    So many heroes,')—seeing he shall treat
The deeds of souls heroic toward the true—
    The oracles of life—previsions sweet
And awful, like divine swans gliding through
    White arms of Ledas, which will leave the heat
Of their escaping godship to endue
    The human medium with a heavenly flush.

Meanwhile, in this same Italy we want
    Not popular passion, to arise and crush,
But popular conscience, which may covenant
    For what it knows. Concede without a blush,
To grant the 'civic guard' is not to grant
    The civic spirit, living and awake.
Those lappets on your shoulders, citizens,
    Your eyes strain after sideways till they ache,
(While still, in admirations and amens,
    The crowd comes up on festa-days, to take
The great sight in)—are not intelligence,
    Not courage even—alas, if not the sign
Of something very noble, they are nought;
    For every day ye dress your sallow kine
With fringes down their cheeks, though unbesought
    They loll their heavy heads and drag the wine,
And bear the wooden yoke as they were taught
    The first day. What ye want is light—indeed
Not sunlight—(ye may well look up surprised
    To those unfathomable heavens that feed
Your purple hills!)—but God's light organised
    In some high soul, crowned capable to lead
The conscious people, conscious and advised,—
    For if we lift a people like mere clay,
It falls the same. We want thee, O unfound
    And sovran teacher!—if thy beard be grey

Or black, we bid thee rise up from the ground
    And speak the word God giveth thee to say,
Inspiring into all this people round,
    Instead of passion, thought, which pioneers
All generous passion, purifies from sin,
    And strikes the hour for. Rise up teacher! here's
A crowd to make a nation!—best begin
    By making each a man, till all be peers
Of earth's true patriots and pure martyrs in
    Knowing and daring. Best unbar the doors
Which Peter's heirs keep locked so overclose
    They only let the mice across the floors,
While every churchman dangles, as he goes,
    The great key at his girdle, and abhors
In Christ's name, meekly. Open wide the house,
    Concede the entrance with Christ's liberal mind,
And set the tables with His wine and bread.
    What! 'commune in both kinds?' In every kind—
Wine, wafer, love, hope, truth, unlimited,
    Nothing kept back. For when a man is blind
To starlight, will he see the rose is red?
    A bondsman shivering at a Jesuit's foot—
'Væ! meâ culpâ!' is not like to stand
    A freedman at a despot's, and dispute
His titles by the balance in his hand,
    Weighing them 'suo jure.' Tend the root
If careful of the branches, and expand
    The inner souls of men before you strive
For civic heroes.

                    But the teacher, where?
    From all these crowded faces, all alive,
Eyes, of their own lids flashing themselves bare,
    And brows that with a mobile life contrive
A deeper shadow,—may we in no wise dare
    To put a finger out, and touch a man,

And cry 'this is the leader?' What, all these!—
 Broad heads, black eyes,—yet not a soul that ran
From God down with a message? all, to please
 The donna waving measures with her fan,
And not the judgment-angel on his knees,
 (The trumpet just an inch off from his lips)
Who when he breathes next, will put out the sun?

 Yet mankind's self were foundered in eclipse,
If lacking doers, with great works to be done;
 And lo, the startled earth already dips
Back into light—a better day's begun—
 And soon this leader, teacher, will stand plain,
And build the golden pipes and synthesize
 This people-organ for a holy strain.
We hold this hope, and still in all these eyes,
 Go sounding for the deep look which shall drain
Suffused thought into channelled enterprise.
 Where is the teacher? What now may he do,
Who shall do greatly? Doth he gird his waist
 With a monk's rope, like Luther? or pursue
The goat, like Tell? or dry his nets in haste,
 Like Masaniello when the sky was blue?
Keep house, like other peasants, with inlaced,
 Bare, brawny arms about a favourite child,
And meditative looks beyond the door,
 (But not to mark the kidling's teeth have filed
The green shoots of his vine which last year bore
 Full twenty bunches,) or, on triple-piled
Throne-velvets sit at ease, to bless the poor,
 Like other pontiffs, in the Poorest's name?
The old tiara keeps itself aslope
 Upon his steady brows, which, all the same,
Bend mildly to permit the people's hope?

Whatever hand shall grasp this oriflamme,
Whatever man (last peasant or first pope
    Seeking to free his country!) shall appear,
Teach, lead, strike fire into the masses, fill
    These empty bladders with fine air, insphere
These wills into a unity of will,
    And make of Italy a nation—dear
And blessed be that man! the Heavens shall kill
    No leaf the earth lets grow for him, and Death
Shall cast him back upon the lap of Life
    To live more surely, in a clarion-breath
Of hero-music. Brutus, with the knife,
    Rienzi, with the fasces, throb beneath
Rome's stones,—and more,—who threw away joy's fife
    Like Pallas, that the beauty of their souls
Might ever shine untroubled and entire.
    But if it can be true that he who rolls
The Church's thunders, will reserve her fire
    For only light,—from eucharistic bowls
Will pour new life for nations that expire,
    And rend the scarlet of his papal vest
To gird the weak loins of his countrymen—
    I hold that he surpasses all the rest
Of Romans, heroes, patriots,—and that when
    He sat down on the throne, he dispossessed
The first graves of some glory. See again,
    This country-saving is a glorious thing,
And if a common man achieved it? well.
    Say, a rich man did? excellent. A king?
That grows sublime. A priest? improbable.
    A pope? Ah, there we stop, and cannot bring
Our faith up to the leap, with history's bell
    So heavy round the neck of it—albeit
We fain would grant the possibility,
    For *thy* sake, Pio nono!

Stretch thy feet
In that case—I will kiss them reverently
    As any pilgrim to the papal seat!
And, such proved possible, thy throne to me
    Shall seem as holy a place as Pellico's
Venetian dungeon, or as Spielberg's grate,
    At which the Lombard woman hung the rose
Of her sweet soul, by its own dewy weight,
    To feel the dungeon round her sunshine close,
And pining so, died early, yet too late
    For what she suffered. Yea, I will not choose
Betwixt thy throne, Pope Pius, and the spot
    Marked red for ever, spite of rains and dews,
Where two fell riddled by the Austrian's shot,
    The brothers Bandiera, who accuse,
With one same mother-voice and face (that what
    They speak may be invincible) the sins
Of earth's tormentors before God the just,
    Until the unconscious thunder-bolt begins
To loosen in His grasp.

                            And yet we must
    Beware, and mark the natural kiths and kins
Of circumstance and office, and distrust
    The rich man reasoning in a poor man's hut,
The poet who neglects pure truth to prove
    Statistic fact, the child who leaves a rut
For a smoother road, the priest who vows his glove
    Exhales no grace, the prince who walks a-foot,
The woman who has sworn she will not love,
    And this Ninth Pius in Seventh Gregory's chair,
With Andrea Doria's forehead!

                            Count what goes
    To making up a pope, before he wear
That triple crown. We pass the world-wide throes

Which went to make the popedom,—the despair
Of free men, good men, wise men; the dread shows
    Of women's faces, by the faggot's flash,
Tossed out, to the minutest stir and throb
    O' the white lips, the least tremble of a lash,
To glut the red stare of a licensed mob;
    The short mad cries down oubliettes, and plash
So horribly far off; priests, trained to rob,
    And kings that, like encouraged nightmares, sate
On nations' hearts most heavily distressed
    With monstrous sights and apophthegms of fate!—
We pass these things,—because 'the times' are prest
    With necessary charges of the weight
Of all this sin, and 'Calvin, for the rest,
    Made bold to burn Servetus—Ah, men err!'—
And, so do *churches!* which is all we mean
    To bring to proof in any register
Of theological fat kine and lean—
    So drive them back into the pens! refer
Old sins (with pourpoint, 'quotha' and 'I ween,')
    Entirely to the old times, the old times;
Nor ever ask why this preponderant,
    Infallible, pure Church could set her chimes
Most loudly then, just then,—most jubilant,
    Precisely then—when mankind stood in crimes
Full heart-deep, and Heaven's judgments were not scant.
    Inquire still less, what signifies a church
Of perfect inspiration and pure laws,
    Who burns the first man with a brimstone-torch,
And grinds the second, bone by bone, because
    The times, forsooth, are used to rack and scorch!
What *is* a holy Church, unless she awes
    The times down from their sins? Did Christ select
Such amiable times, to come and teach
    Love to, and mercy? The whole world were wrecked,
If every mere great man, who lives to reach

A little leaf of popular respect,
Attained not simply by some special breach
    In the age's customs, by some precedence
In thought and act, which, having proved him higher
    Than those he lived with, proved his competence
In helping them to wonder and aspire.

My words are guiltless of the bigot's sense.
My soul has fire to mingle with the fire
    Of all these souls, within or out of doors
Of Rome's church or another. I believe
    In one Priest, and one temple, with its floors
Of shining jasper gloom'd at morn and eve
    By countless knees of earnest auditors,
And crystal walls, too lucid to perceive,
    That none may take the measure of the place
And say, 'So far the porphyry, then, the flint—
    To this mark, mercy goes, and there, ends grace,'
Though still the permeable crystals hint
    At some white starry distance, bathed in space.
I feel how nature's ice-crusts keep the dint
    Of undersprings of silent Deity.
I hold the articulated gospels, which
    Show Christ among us, crucified on tree.
I love all who love truth, if poor or rich
    In what they have won of truth possessively.
No altars and no hands defiled with pitch
    Shall scare me off, but I will pray and eat
With all these—taking leave to choose my ewers
    And say at last, 'Your visible churches cheat
Their inward types,—and, if a church assures
    Of standing without failure and defeat,
The same both fails and lies.'

                              To leave which lures
Of wider subject through past years,—behold,
We come back from the popedom to the pope,
    To ponder what he *must* be, ere we are bold
For what he *may* be, with our heavy hope
    To trust upon his soul. So, fold by fold,
Explore this mummy in the priestly cope,
    Transmitted through the darks of time, to catch
The man within the wrappage, and discern
    How he, an honest man, upon the watch
Full fifty years, for what a man may learn,
    Contrived to get just there; with what a snatch
Of old-world oboli he had to earn
    The passage through; with what a drowsy sop,
To drench the busy barkings of his brain;
    What ghosts of pale tradition, wreathed with hop
'Gainst wakeful thought, he had to entertain
    For heavenly visions; and consent to stop
The clock at noon, and let the hour remain
    (Without vain windings up) inviolate,
Against all chimings from the belfry. Lo,
    From every given pope you must abate,
Albeit you love him, some things—good, you know—
    Which every given heretic you hate,
Assumes for his, as being plainly so.
    A pope must hold by popes a little,—yes,
By councils,—from Nicæa up to Trent,—
    By hierocratic empire, more or less
Irresponsible to men,—he must resent
    Each man's particular conscience, and repress
Inquiry, meditation, argument,
    As tyrants faction. Also, he must not
Love truth too dangerously, but prefer
    'The interests of the Church,' (because a blot
Is better than a rent, in miniver)
    Submit to see the people swallow hot

Husk-porridge, which his chartered churchmen stir
  Quoting the only true God's epigraph,
'Feed my lambs, Peter!'—must consent to sit
  Attesting with his pastoral ring and staff,
To such a picture of our Lady, hit
  Off well by artist angels, (though not half
As fair as Giotto would have painted it)—
  To such a vial, where a dead man's blood
Runs yearly warm beneath a churchman's finger;
  To such a holy house of stone and wood,
Whereof a cloud of angels was the bringer
  From Bethlehem to Loreto.—Were it good
For any pope on earth to be a flinger
  Of stones against these high-niched counterfeits?
Apostates only are iconoclasts.
  He dares not say, while this false thing abets
That true thing, 'this is false.' He keeps his fasts
  And prayers, as prayer and fast were silver frets
To change a note upon a string that lasts,
  And make a lie a virtue. Now, if he
Did more than this, higher hoped, and braver dared,
  I think he were a pope in jeopardy,
Or no pope rather, for his truth had barred
  The vaulting of his life,—and certainly,
If he do only this, mankind's regard
  Moves on from him at once, to seek some new
Teacher and leader. He is good and great
  According to the deeds a pope can do;
Most liberal, save those bonds; affectionate,
  As princes may be, and, as priests are, true;
But only the ninth Pius after eight,
  When all's praised most. At best and hopefullest,
He's pope—we want a man! his heart beats warm,
  But, like the prince enchanted to the waist,
He sits in stone, and hardens by a charm
  Into the marble of his throne high-placed.

Mild benediction, waves his saintly arm—
    So, good! but what we want's a perfect man,
Complete and all alive: half travertine
    Half suits our need, and ill subserves our plan.
Feet, knees, nerves, sinews, energies divine
    Were never yet too much for men who ran
In such hard ways as must be this of thine,
    Deliverer whom we seek, whoe'er thou art,
Pope, prince, or peasant! If, indeed, the first,
    The noblest, therefore! since the heroic heart
Within thee must be great enough to burst
    Those trammels buckling to the baser part
Thy saintly peers in Rome, who crossed and cursed
    With the same finger.

                              Come, appear, be found,
If pope or peasant, come! we hear the cock,
    The courtier of the mountains when first crowned
With golden dawn; and orient glories flock
    To meet the sun upon the highest ground.
Take voice and work! we wait to hear thee knock
    At some one of our Florentine nine gates,
On each of which was imaged a sublime
    Face of a Tuscan genius, which, for hate's
And love's sake, both, our Florence in her prime
    Turned boldly on all comers to her states,
As heroes turned their shields in antique time,
    Emblazoned with honourable acts. And though
The gates are blank now of such images,
    And Petrarch looks no more from Nicolo
Toward dear Arezzo, 'twixt the acacia trees,
    Nor Dante, from gate Gallo—still we know,
Despite the razing of the blazonries,
    Remains the consecration of the shield!
The dead heroic faces will start out
    On all these gates, if foes should take the field,

And blend sublimely, at the earliest shout,
    With living heroes who will scorn to yield
A hair's-breadth even, when gazing round about,
    They find in what a glorious company
They fight the foes of Florence. Who will grudge
    His one poor life, when that great man we see
Has given five hundred years, the world being judge,
    To help the glory of his Italy?
Who, born the fair side of the Alps, will budge,
    When Dante stays, when Ariosto stays,
When Petrarch stays for ever? Ye bring swords,
    My Tuscans? Ay, if wanted in this haze,
Bring swords. But first bring souls!—bring thoughts
    and words,
    Unrusted by a tear of yesterday's,
Yet awful by its wrong,—and cut these cords,
    And mow this green lush falseness to the roots,
And shut the mouth of hell below the swathe!
    And, if ye can bring songs too, let the lute's
Recoverable music softly bathe
    Some poet's hand, that, through all bursts and bruits
Of popular passion, all unripe and rathe
    Convictions of the popular intellect,
Ye may not lack a finger up the air,
    Annunciative, reproving, pure, erect,
To show which way your first Ideal bare
    The whiteness of its wings, when (sorely pecked
By falcons on your wrists) it unaware
    Arose up overhead, and out of sight.

Meanwhile, let all the far ends of the world
    Breathe back the deep breath of their old delight,
To swell the Italian banner just unfurled.
    Help, lands of Europe! for, if Austria fight,
The drums will bar your slumber. Had ye curled
    The laurel for your thousand artists' brows,

If these Italian hands had planted none?
    Can any sit down idle in the house,
Nor hear appeals from Buonarroti's stone
    And Raffael's canvas, rousing and to rouse?
Where's Poussin's master? Gallic Avignon
    Bred Laura, and Vaucluse's fount has stirred
The heart of France too strongly, as it lets
    Its little stream out, (like a wizard's bird
Which bounds upon its emerald wing and wets
    The rocks on each side) that she should not gird
Her loins with Charlemagne's sword when foes beset
    The country of her Petrarch. Spain may well
Be minded how from Italy she caught,
    To mingle with her tinkling Moorish bell,
A fuller cadence and a subtler thought.
    And even the New World, the receptacle
Of freemen, may send glad men, as it ought,
    To greet Vespucci Amerigo's door.
While England claims, by trump of poetry,
    Verona, Venice, the Ravenna-shore,
And dearer holds John Milton's Fiesole
    Than Langlande's Malvern with the stars in flower.

And Vallombrosa, we two went to see
    Last June, beloved companion,—where sublime
The mountains live in holy families,
    And the slow pinewoods ever climb and climb
Half up their breasts, just stagger as they seize
    Some grey crag, drop back with it many a time,
And straggle blindly down the precipice!
    The Vallombrosan brooks were strewn as thick
That June-day, knee-deep, with dead beechen leaves,
    As Milton saw them, ere his heart grew sick
And his eyes blind. I think the monks and beeves
    Are all the same too. Scarce they have changed the
    wick

On good St. Gualbert's altar, which receives
　　The convent's pilgrims,—and the pool in front
(Wherein the hill-stream trout are cast, to wait
　　The beatific vision and the grunt
Used at refectory) keeps its weedy state,
　　To baffle saintly abbots who would count
The fish across their breviary nor 'bate
　　The measure of their steps. O waterfalls
And forests! sound and silence! mountains bare,
　　That leap up peak by peak, and catch the palls
Of purple and silver mist to rend and share
　　With one another, at electric calls
Of life in the sunbeams,—till we cannot dare
　　Fix your shapes, count your number! we must think
Your beauty and your glory helped to fill
　　The cup of Milton's soul so to the brink,
He never more was thirsty, when God's will
　　Had shattered to his sense the last chain-link
By which he had drawn from Nature's visible
　　The fresh well-water. Satisfied by this,
He sang of Adam's paradise and smiled,
　　Remembering Vallombrosa. Therefore is
The place divine to English man and child,
　　And pilgrims leave their souls here in a kiss.

For Italy's the whole earth's treasury, piled
　　With reveries of gentle ladies, flung
Aside, like ravelled silk, from life's worn stuff;
　　With coins of scholars' fancy, which, being rung
On work-day counter, still sound silver-proof;
　　In short, with all the dreams of dreamers young,
Before their heads have time for slipping off
　　Hope's pillow to the ground. How oft, indeed,
We've sent our souls out from the rigid north,
　　On bare white feet which would not print nor bleed,
To climb the Alpine passes and look forth,

Where booming low the Lombard rivers lead
To gardens, vineyards, all a dream is worth,—
    Sights, thou and I, Love, have seen afterward
From Tuscan Bellosguardo, wide awake,
    When, standing on the actual blessed sward
Where Galileo stood at nights to take
    The vision of the stars, we have found it hard,
Gazing upon the earth and heaven, to make
    A choice of beauty.

                                    Therefore let us all
Refreshed in England or in other land,
    By visions, with their fountain-rise and fall,
Of this earth's darling,—we, who understand
    A little how the Tuscan musical
Vowels do round themselves as if they planned
    Eternities of separate sweetness,—we,
Who loved Sorrento vines in picture-book,
    Or ere in wine-cup we pledged faith or glee,—
Who loved Rome's wolf, with demi-gods at suck,
    Or ere we loved truth's own divinity,—
Who loved, in brief, the classic hill and brook,
    And Ovid's dreaming tales, and Petrarch's song,
Or ere we loved Love's self even!—let us give
    The blessing of our souls, (and wish them strong
To bear it to the height where prayers arrive,
    When faithful spirits pray against a wrong,)
To this great cause of southern men, who strive
    In God's name for man's rights, and shall not fail!

Behold, they shall not fail. The shouts ascend
    Above the shrieks, in Naples, and prevail.
Rows of shot corpses, waiting for the end
    Of burial, seem to smile up straight and pale
Into the azure air and apprehend
    That final gun-flash from Palermo's coast

Which lightens their apocalypse of death.
    So let them die! The world shows nothing lost;
Therefore, not blood. Above or underneath,
    What matter, brothers, if ye keep your post
On duty's side? As sword returns to sheath,
    So dust to grave, but souls find place in Heaven.
Heroic daring is the true success,
    The eucharistic bread requires no leaven;
And though your ends were hopeless, we should bless
    Your cause as holy. Strive—and, having striven,
Take, for God's recompense, that righteousness!

Poems Selected from

POEMS BEFORE CONGRESS
(1860)

Preface

Elizabeth Barrett Browning referred to this volume as "a very thin and wicked brochure on Italian affairs" and predicted "everyone will hate me for it". She was right. The poems were condemned as "trite" by *Blackwood's*, who implied that she was ill-equipped to write on Italian politics. So did her brother George. She resented this assumption and wrote sharply to her brother that she might be wrong in her opinions but that she was not ignorant.

"A Curse for a Nation" had nothing to do with Italian affairs and was out of place in this volume. It was an attack on slavery, written in 1856 for an American magazine, the Boston *Liberty Bell*. Henry Chorley, reviewing it in *The Athenaeum*, interpreted it (with some justification) as an attack on England's refusal to assist the cause of Italian liberalism. It is one of Elizabeth Barrett Browning's strongest political poems: she speaks out, as she wished to, about women's duty to involve themselves more in direct action and not to hide behind their supposed frailty.

The title of this volume refers to a congress which never took place. Napoleon III, after the Treaty of Villafranca, invited the European powers to a congress in Paris to discuss the provisions of the treaty, but events intervened and it was never held. Elizabeth Barrett Browning, believing the congress to be merely postponed, kept her title.

A CURSE FOR A NATION

PROLOGUE

I heard an angel speak last night,
    And he said 'Write!
Write a Nation's curse for me,
And send it over the Western Sea.'

I faltered, taking up the word:
    'Not so, my lord!
If curses must be, choose another
To send thy curse against my brother.

'For I am bound by gratitude,
    By love and blood,
To brothers of mine across the sea,
Who stretch out kindly hands to me.'

'Therefore,' the voice said, 'shalt thou write
    My curse to-night.
From the summits of love a curse is driven,
As lightning is from the tops of heaven.'

'Not so,' I answered. 'Evermore
    My heart is sore
For my own land's sins: for little feet
Of children bleeding along the street:

'For parked-up honours that gainsay
    The right of way:
For almsgiving through a door that is
Not open enough for two friends to kiss:

'For love of freedom which abates
        Beyond the Straits:
For patriot virtue starved to vice on
Self-praise, self-interest, and suspicion:

'For an oligarchic parliament,
        And bribes well-meant.
What curse to another land assign,
When heavy-souled for the sins of mine?'

'Therefore,' the voice said, 'shalt thou write
        My curse to-night.
Because thou hast strength to see and hate
A foul thing done *within* thy gate.'

'Not so,' I answered once again.
        'To curse, choose men.
For I, a woman, have only known
How the heart melts and the tears run down.'

'Therefore,' the voice said, 'shalt thou write
        My curse to-night.
Some women weep and curse, I say
(And no one marvels), night and day.

'And thou shalt take their part to-night,
        Weep and write.
A curse from the depths of womanhood
Is very salt, and bitter, and good.'

So thus I wrote, and mourned indeed,
        What all may read.
And thus, as was enjoined on me,
I send it over the Western Sea.

THE CURSE

I

Because ye have broken your own chain
    With the strain
Of brave men climbing a Nation's height,
Yet thence bear down with brand and thong
On souls of others,—for this wrong
    This is the curse. Write.

Because yourselves are standing straight
    In the state
Of Freedom's foremost acolyte,
Yet keep calm footing all the time
On writhing bond-slaves,—for this crime
    This is the curse. Write.

Because ye prosper in God's name,
    With a claim
To honour in the old world's sight,
Yet do the fiend's work perfectly
In strangling martyrs,—for this lie
    This is the curse. Write.

II

Ye shall watch while kings conspire
Round the people's smouldering fire,
    And, warm for your part,
Shall never dare—O shame!
To utter the thought into flame
    Which burns at your heart.
      This is the curse. Write.

Ye shall watch while nations strive
With the bloodhounds, die or survive,
　　Drop faint from their jaws,
Or throttle them backward to death,
And only under your breath
　　Shall favour the cause.
　　　　This is the curse. Write.

Ye shall watch while strong men draw
The nets of feudal law
　　To strangle the weak,
And, counting the sin for a sin,
Your soul shall be sadder within
　　Than the word ye shall speak.
　　　　This is the curse. Write.

When good men are praying erect
That Christ may avenge His elect
　　And deliver the earth,
The prayer in your ears, said low,
Shall sound like the tramp of a foe
　　That's driving you forth.
　　　　This is the curse. Write.

When wise men give you their praise,
They shall pause in the heat of the phrase,
　　As if carried too far.
When ye boast your own charters kept true,
Ye shall blush;—for the thing which ye do
　　Derives what ye are.
　　　　This is the curse. Write.

When fools cast taunts at your gate,
Your scorn ye shall somewhat abate
   As ye look o'er the wall,
For your conscience, tradition, and name
Explode with a deadlier blame
   Than the worst of them all.
       This is the curse. Write.

Go, wherever ill deeds shall be done,
Go, plant your flag in the sun
   Beside the ill-doers!
And recoil from clenching the curse
Of God's witnessing Universe
   With a curse of yours.
       THIS is the curse. Write.

A COURT LADY

I

Her hair was tawny with gold, her
   eyes with purple were dark,
Her cheeks' pale opal burnt with a red
   and restless spark.

II

Never was lady of Milan nobler in name
   and in race;
Never was lady of Italy fairer to see in
   the face.

III

Never was lady on earth more true as
   woman and wife,
Larger in judgement and instinct, prouder
   in manners and life.

IV

She stood in the early morning, and
    said to her maidens, 'Bring
That silken robe made ready to wear at
    the court of the king.

V

'Bring me the clasps of diamond, lucid,
    clear of the mote,
Clasp me the large at the waist, and
    clasp me the small at the throat.

VI

'Diamonds to fasten the hair, and
    diamonds to fasten the sleeves,
Laces to drop from their rays, like
    a powder of snow from the eaves.'

VII

Gorgeous she entered the sunlight
    which gathered her up in a flame,
While, straight in her open carriage,
    she to the hospital came.

VIII

In she went at the door, and gazing
    from end to end,
'Many and low are the pallets, but
    each is the place of a friend.'

IX

Up she passed through the wards, and
    stood at a young man's bed:
Bloody the band on his brow, and livid
    the droop of his head.

X

'Art thou a Lombard, my brother?
  Happy art thou,' she cried,
And smiled like Italy on him: he
  dreamed in her face and died.

XI

Pale with his passing soul, she went on
  still to a second:
He was a grave hard man, whose years
  by dungeons were reckoned.

XII

Wounds in his body were sore, wounds
  in his life were sorer.
'Art thou a Romagnole?' Her eyes
  drove lightnings before her.

XIII

'Austrian and priest had joined to double
  and tighten the cord
Able to bind thee, O strong one,—free
  by the stroke of a sword.

XIV

'Now be grave for the rest of us, using
  the life overcast
To ripen our wine of the present, (too
  new,) in glooms of the past.'

XV

Down she stepped to a pallet where lay
  a face like a girl's,
Young, and pathetic with dying,—a deep
  black hole in the curls.

XVI

'Art thou from Tuscany, brother? and
    seest thou, dreaming in pain,
Thy mother stand in the piazza, search-
    ing the List of the slain?'

XVII

Kind as a mother herself, she touched
    his cheeks with her hands:
'Blessed is she who has borne thee,
    although she should weep as she stands.'

XVIII

On she passed to a Frenchman, his arm
    carried off by a ball:
Kneeling, . . 'O more than my brother!
    how shall I thank thee for all?

XIX

'Each of the heroes around us has fought
    for his land and line,
But *thou* hast fought for a stranger, in
    hate of a wrong not thine.

XX

'Happy are all free peoples, too strong
    to be dispossessed.
But blessed are those among nations, who
    dare to be strong for the rest!'

XXI

Ever she passed on her way, and came
    to a couch where pined
One with a face from Venetia, white with
    a hope out of mind.

XXII

Long she stood and gazed, and twice she
      tried at the name,
But two great crystal tears were all that
      faltered and came.

XXIII

Only a tear for Venice?—she turned as
      in passion and loss,
And stooped to his forehead and kissed
      it, as if she were kissing the cross.

XXIV

Faint with that strain of heart she moved
      on then to another,
Stern and strong in his death. 'And
      dost thou suffer, my brother?'

XXV

Holding his hands in hers:—'Out of the
      Piedmont lion
Cometh the sweetness of freedom!
      sweetest to live or to die on.'

XXVI

Holding his cold rough hands,—'Well,
      oh, well have ye done
In noble, noble Piedmont, who would
      not be noble alone.'

XXVII

Back he fell while she spoke. She rose
      to her feet with a spring,—
'That was a Piedmontese! and this is
      the Court of the King.'

A TALE OF VILLAFRANCA

I

My little son, my Florentine,
  Sit down beside my knee,
And I will tell you why the sign
  Of joy which flushed our Italy,
Has faded since but yesternight;
And why your Florence of delight
  Is mourning as you see.

II

A great man (who was crowned one day)
  Imagined a great Deed:
He shaped it out of cloud and clay,
  He touched it finely till the seed
Possessed the flower: from heart and brain
He fed it with large thoughts humane,
  To help a people's need.

III

He brought it out into the sun—
  They blessed it to his face:
'O great pure Deed, that hast undone
  So many bad and base!
O generous Deed, heroic Deed,
Come forth, be perfected, succeed,
  Deliver by God's grace.'

IV

Then sovereigns, statesmen, north and south,
   Rose up in wrath and fear,
And cried, protesting by one mouth,
   'What monster have we here?
A great Deed at this hour of day?
A great just Deed—and not for pay?
    Absurd,—or insincere.

V

'And if sincere, the heavier blow
   In that case we shall bear,
For where's our blessed "status quo,"
   Our holy treaties, where,—
Our rights to sell a race, or buy,
Protect and pillage, occupy,
    And civilize despair?'

VI

Some muttered that the great Deed meant
   A great pretext to sin;
And others, the pretext, so lent,
   Was heinous (to begin).
Volcanic terms of 'great' and 'just'?
Admit such tongues of flame, the crust
    Of time and law falls in.

VII

A great Deed in this world of ours?
   Unheard of the pretence is:
It threatens plainly the great Powers;
   Is fatal in all senses.
A just Deed in the world?—call out
The rifles! be not slack about
    The national defences.

VIII

And many murmured, 'From this source
    What red blood must be poured!'
And some rejoined, ''Tis even worse;
    What red tape is ignored!'
All cursed the Doer for an evil
Called here, enlarging on the Devil,—
    There, monkeying the Lord!

IX

Some said, it could not be explained,
    Some, could not be excused;
And others, 'Leave it unrestrained,
    Gehenna's self is loosed.'
And all cried, 'Crush it, maim it, gag it!
Set dog-toothed lies to tear it ragged,
    Truncated and traduced!'

X

But HE stood sad before the sun
    (The peoples felt their fate).
'The world is many,—I am one;
    My great Deed was too great.
God's fruit of justice ripens slow:
Men's souls are narrow; let them grow.
    My brothers, we must wait.'

XI

The tale is ended, child of mine,
    Turned graver at my knee.
They say your eyes, my Florentine,
    Are English: it may be:
And yet I've marked as blue a pair
Following the doves across the square
    At Venice by the sea.

XII

Ah, child! ah, child! I cannot say
    A word more. You conceive
The reason now, why just to-day
    We see our Florence grieve.
Ah, child, look up into the sky!
In this low world, where great Deeds die,
    What matter if we live?

THE DANCE

I

You remember down at Florence our Cascine,
    Where the people on the feast-days walk and drive,
And, through the trees, long-drawn in many a green way,
    O'er-roofing hum and murmur like a hive,
    The river and the mountains look alive?

II

You remember the piazzone there, the stand-place
    Of carriages a-brim with Florence Beauties,
Who lean and melt to music as the band plays,
    Or smile and chat with some one who afoot is,
    Or on horseback, in observance of male duties?

III

'Tis so pretty, in the afternoons of summer,
    So many gracious faces brought together!
Call it rout, or call it concert, they have come here,
    In the floating of the fan and of the feather,
    To reciprocate with beauty the fine weather.

IV

While the flower-girls offer nosegays (because *they* too
　　Go with other sweets) at every carriage-door;
Here, by shake of a white finger, signed away to
　　Some next buyer, who sits buying score on score,
　　Piling roses upon roses evermore.

V

And last season, when the French camp had its station
　　In the meadow-ground, things quickened and grew gayer
Through the mingling of the liberating nation
　　With this people; groups of Frenchmen everywhere,
　　Strolling, gazing, judging lightly . . 'who was fair.'

VI

Then the noblest lady present took upon her
　　To speak nobly from her carriage for the rest;
'Pray these officers from France to do us honour
　　By dancing with us straightway.'—The request
　　Was gravely apprehended as addressed.

VII

And the men of France bareheaded, bowing lowly,
　　Led out each a proud signora to the space
Which the startled crowd had rounded for them—slowly,
　　Just a touch of still emotion in his face,
　　Not presuming, through the symbol, on the grace.

VIII

There was silence in the people: some lips trembled,
　　But none jested. Broke the music, at a glance:
And the daughters of our princes, thus assembled,
　　Stepped the measure with the gallant sons of France.
　　Hush! it might have been a Mass, and not a dance.

IX

And they danced there till the blue that overskied us
  Swooned with passion, though the footing seemed sedate;
And the mountains, heaving mighty hearts beside us,
  Sighed a rapture in a shadow, to dilate,
  And touch the holy stone where Dante sate.

X

Then the sons of France bareheaded, lowly bowing,
  Led the ladies back where kinsmen of the south
Stood, received them;—till, with burst of overflowing
  Feeling . . husbands, brothers, Florence's male youth,
  Turned, and kissed the martial strangers mouth to mouth.

XI

And a cry went up, a cry from all that people!
  —You have heard a people cheering, you suppose,
For the Member, Mayor . . with chorus from the steeple?
  This was different: scarce as loud perhaps (who knows?),
  For we saw wet eyes around us ere the close.

XII

And we felt as if a nation, too long borne in
  By hard wrongers, comprehending in such attitude
That God had spoken somewhere since the morning,
  That men were somehow brothers, by no platitude,
  Cried exultant in great wonder and free gratitude.

CHRISTMAS GIFTS

ὡς βασιλεῖ, ὡς θεῷ, ὡς νεκρῷ.
GREGORY NAZIANZEN

I

The Pope on Christmas Day
　Sits in St. Peter's chair;
But the peoples murmur and say,
　'Our souls are sick and forlorn,
And who will show us where
　Is the stable where Christ was born?'

II

The star is lost in the dark;
　The manger is lost in the straw;
The Christ cries faintly . . hark! . .
　Through bands that swaddle and
　　　strangle—
But the Pope in the chair of awe
　Looks down the great quadrangle.

III

The magi kneel at his foot,
　Kings of the east and west,
But, instead of the angels (mute
　Is the 'Peace on earth' of their song),
The peoples, perplexed and opprest,
　Are sighing, 'How long, how long?'

IV

And, instead of the kine, bewilder in
　Shadow of aisle and dome,
The bear who tore up the children,
　The fox who burnt up the corn,
And the wolf who suckled at Rome
　Brothers to slay and to scorn.

V

Cardinals left and right of him,
  Worshippers round and beneath,
The silver trumpets at sight of him
  Thrill with a musical blast:
But the people say through their teeth,
  'Trumpets? we wait for the Last!'

VI

He sits in the place of the Lord,
  And asks for the gifts of the time;
Gold, for the haft of a sword,
  To win back Romagna averse,
Incense, to sweeten a crime,
  And myrrh, to embitter a curse.

VII

Then a king of the west said, 'Good!—
  I bring thee the gifts of the time;
Red, for the patriot's blood,
  Green, for the martyr's crown,
White, for the dew and the rime,
  When the morning of God comes
    down.'

VIII

—O mystic tricolor bright!
  The Pope's heart quailed like a man's:
The cardinals froze at the sight,
  Bowing their tonsures hoary:
And the eyes in the peacock-fans
  Winked at the alien glory.

IX

But the peoples exclaimed in hope,
   'Now blessed be he who has brought
These gifts of the time to the Pope,
   When our souls were sick and forlorn.
—And *here* is the star we sought,
   To show us where Christ was born!'

Poems Selected from

LAST POEMS
(1862)

Preface

After Elizabeth Barrett Browning's death, on 29th June 1861, it was some small comfort for Robert Browning to arrange the publication of many poems which had not yet appeared in any form.

"Lord Walter's Wife" was written for Thackeray's new *Cornhill Magazine* but was rejected by him, with considerable embarrassment, as too daring for family consumption. It was an attack on the "double standard" by which men could flirt and were thought amusing, and women flirt only to be condemned as wanton. In other poems—"Amy's Cruelty", "A False Step", "Void in Law"—Elizabeth Barrett Browning has equally strong opinions to express on different aspects of this "double standard". She would prefer society to change its habits of courtship, so that vows of love would become sincere, but until it did she warned women to resist exploitation.

While warning women of love's pitfalls, she also reaffirms its power and beauty. "Bianca among the Nightingales" celebrates sexual passion and "My Heart and I" doubts if a life without love is worth anything.

Robert Browning found a place for his wife's political verse, too. After *Casa Guidi Windows* and *Poems Before Congress*, she had by no means done with what she called "rushing into the fire". Her pity for young Italian conscripts produced "The Forced Recruit", and in "First News from Villafranca" she attacked the spirit of aggrandisement which had motivated the war in which they died. Her feeling for those women who had lost sons was evident in "Mother and Poet".

LORD WALTER'S WIFE

I

'But why do you go,' said the lady, while both sat under the
     yew,
And her eyes were alive in their depth, as the kraken beneath
     the sea-blue.

II

'Because I fear you,' he answered;—'because you are far too
     fair,
And able to strangle my soul in a mesh of your gold-coloured
     hair.'

III

'Oh, that,' she said, 'is no reason! Such knots are quickly
     undone,
And too much beauty, I reckon, is nothing but too much sun.'

IV

'Yet farewell so,' he answered;—'the sun-stroke's fatal at
     times.
I value your husband, Lord Walter, whose gallop rings still
     from the limes.'

V

'Oh, that,' she said, 'is no reason. You smell a rose through a
     fence:
If two should smell it, what matters? who grumbles, and
     where's the pretence?'

VI

'But I,' he replied, 'have promised another, when love was free,
To love her alone, alone, who alone and afar loves me.'

'Why, that,' she said, 'is no reason. Love's always free, I am
    told.
Will you vow to be safe from the headache on Tuesday, and
    think it will hold?'

'But you,' he replied, 'have a daughter, a young little child, who
    was laid
In your lap to be pure; so, I leave you: the angels would make
    me afraid.'

'Oh, that,' she said, 'is no reason. The angels keep out of the
    way;
And Dora, the child, observes nothing, although you should
    please me and stay.'

At which he rose up in his anger,—'Why, now, you no longer
    are fair!
Why, now, you no longer are fatal, but ugly and hateful, I
    swear.'

At which she laughed out in her scorn.—'These men! Oh, these
    men overnice,
Who are shocked if a colour, not virtuous, is frankly put on by a
    vice.'

Her eyes blazed upon him—'And *you!* You bring us your vices
    so near
That we smell them! You think in our presence a thought
    'twould defame us to hear!

XIII

'What reason had you, and what right,—I appeal to your soul
    from my life,—
To find me too fair as a woman? Why, sir, I am pure, and a wife.

XIV

'Is the day-star too fair up above you? It burns you not. Dare
    you imply
I brushed you more close than the star does, when Walter had
    set me as high?

XV

'If a man finds a woman too fair, he means simply adapted too
    much
To uses unlawful and fatal. The praise!—shall I thank you for
    such?

XVI

'Too fair?—not unless you misuse us! and surely if, once in a
    while,
You attain to it, straightway you call us no longer too fair, but
    too vile.

XVII

'A moment? I pray your attention!—I have a poor word in my
    head
I must utter, though womanly custom would set it down better
    unsaid.

XVIII

'You grew, sir, pale to impertinence, once when I showed you a
    ring.
You kissed my fan when I dropped it. No matter!—I've broken
    the thing.

'You did me the honour, perhaps, to be moved at my side now
    and then
In the senses—a vice, I have heard, which is common to beasts
    and some men.

'Love's a virtue for heroes!—as white as the snow on high hills,
And immortal as every great soul is that struggles, endures, and
    fulfils.

'I love my Walter profoundly,—you, Maude, though you
    faltered a week,
For the sake of . . what was it? an eyebrow? or, less still, a mole
    on a cheek?

'And since, when all's said, you're too noble to stoop to the
    frivolous cant
About crimes irresistible, virtues that swindle, betray and
    supplant,

'I determined to prove to yourself that, whate'er you might
    dream or avow
By illusion, you wanted precisely no more of me than you have
    now.

'There! look me full in the face!—in the face. Understand, if
    you can,
That the eyes of such women as I am, are clean as the palm of a
    man.

'Drop his hand, you insult him. Avoid us for fear we should
    cost you a scar—
You take us for harlots, I tell you, and not for the women we
    are.

'You wronged me: but then I considered . . . there's Walter!
    And so at the end,
I vowed that he should not be mulcted, by me, in the hand of a
    friend.

'Have I hurt you indeed? We are quits then. Nay, friend of my
    Walter, be mine!
Come Dora, my darling, my angel, and help me to ask him to
    dine.'

AMY'S CRUELTY

I

Fair Amy of the terraced house,
    Assist me to discover
Why you who would not hurt a mouse
    Can torture so your lover.

II

You give your coffee to the cat,
    You stroke the dog for coming,
And all your face grows kinder at
    The little brown bee's humming.

III

But when *he* haunts your door . . the town
    Marks coming and marks going . .
You seem to have stitched your eyelids down
    To that long piece of sewing!

IV

You never give a look, not you,
    Nor drop him a 'Good-morning,'
To keep his long day warm and blue,
    So fretted by your scorning.

V

She shook her head—'The mouse and bee
    For crumb or flower will linger:
The dog is happy at my knee,
    The cat purrs at my finger.

VI

'But *he* . . to *him*, the least thing given
    Means great things at a distance;
He wants my world, my sun, my heaven,
    Soul, body, whole existence.

VII

'They say love gives as well as takes;
    But I'm a simple maiden,—
My mother's first smile when she wakes
    I still have smiled and prayed in.

VIII

'I only know my mother's love
    Which gives all and asks nothing;
And this new loving sets the groove
    Too much the way of loathing.

IX

'Unless he gives me all in change,
    I forfeit all things by him:
The risk is terrible and strange—
    I tremble, doubt, . . deny him.

X

'He's sweetest friend, or hardest foe,
    Best angel, or worst devil;
I either hate or . . love him so,
    I can't be merely civil!

XI

'You trust a woman who puts forth,
    Her blossoms thick as summer's?
You think she dreams what love is worth,
    Who casts it to new-comers?

XII

'Such love's a cowslip-ball to fling,
    A moment's pretty pastime;
I give . . all me, if anything,
    The first time and the last time.

XIII

'Dear neighbour of the trellised house,
    A man should murmur never,
Though treated worse than dog and mouse,
    Till doted on for ever!'

A FALSE STEP

I

Sweet, thou hast trod on a heart.
  Pass! there's a world full of men,
And women as fair as thou art
  Must do such things now and then.

II

Thou only hast stepped unaware,—
  Malice, not one can impute;
And why should a heart have been there
  In the way of a fair woman's foot?

III

It was not a stone that could trip,
  Nor was it a thorn that could rend:
Put up thy proud underlip!
  'Twas merely the heart of a friend.

IV

And yet peradventure one day
  Thou, sitting alone at the glass,
Remarking the bloom gone away,
  Where the smile in its dimplement was,

V

And seeking around thee in vain
  From hundreds who flattered before,
Such a word as, 'Oh, not in the main
  Do I hold thee less precious, but more!' . . .

Thou'lt sigh, very like, on thy part,
  'Of all I have known or can know,
I wish I had only that Heart
  I trod upon ages ago!'

MY HEART AND I

I

Enough! we're tired, my heart and I.
  We sit beside the headstone thus,
  And wish that name were carved for us.
The moss reprints more tenderly
  The hard types of the mason's knife,
  As Heaven's sweet life renews earth's life
With which we're tired, my heart and I.

II

You see we're tired, my heart and I.
  We dealt with books, we trusted men,
  And in our own blood drenched the pen,
As if such colours could not fly.
  We walked too straight for fortune's end,
  We loved too true to keep a friend;
At last we're tired, my heart and I.

III

How tired we feel, my heart and I!
  We seem of no use in the world;
  Our fancies hang grey and uncurled
About men's eyes indifferently;
  Our voice which thrilled you so, will let
  You sleep; our tears are only wet:
What do we here, my heart and I?

IV

So tired, so tired, my heart and I!
 It was not thus in that old time
 When Ralph sat with me 'neath the lime
To watch the sunset from the sky.
 'Dear love, you're looking tired,' he said
 I, smiling at him, shook my head:
'Tis now we're tired, my heart and I.

V

So tired, so tired, my heart and I!
 Though now none takes me on his arm
 To fold me close and kiss me warm
Till each quick breath end in a sigh
 Of happy languor. Now, alone,
 We lean upon this graveyard stone,
Uncheered, unkissed, my heart and I.

VI

Tired out we are, my heart and I.
 Suppose the world brought diadems
 To tempt us, crusted with loose gems
Of powers and pleasures? Let it try.
 We scarcely care to look at even
 A pretty child, or God's blue heaven,
We feel so tired, my heart and I.

VII

Yet who complains? My heart and I?
 In this abundant earth no doubt
 Is little room for things worn out:
Disdain them, break them, throw them by!
 And if before the days grew rough
 We *once* were loved, used,—well
  enough,
I think, we've fared, my heart and I.

BIANCA AMONG THE NIGHTINGALES

I

The cypress stood up like a church
  That night we felt our love would hold,
And saintly moonlight seemed to search
  And wash the whole world clean as gold;
The olives crystallized the vales'
  Broad slopes until the hills grew strong:
The fireflies and the nightingales
  Throbbed each to either, flame and song.
The nightingales, the nightingales.

II

Upon the angle of its shade
  The cypress stood, self-balanced high;
Half up, half down, as double made,
  Along the ground, against the sky.
And *we* too! from such soul-height went
  Such leaps of blood, so blindly driven,
We scarce knew if our nature meant
  Most passionate earth or intense heaven.
The nightingales, the nightingales.

III

We paled with love, we shook with love,
  We kissed so close we could not vow;
Till Giulio whispered, 'Sweet, above
  God's Ever guarantees this Now.'
And through his words the nightingales
  Drove straight and full their long clear call,
Like arrows through heroic mails,
  And love was awful in it all.
The nightingales, the nightingales.

IV

O cold white moonlight of the north,
    Refresh these pulses, quench this hell!
O coverture of death drawn forth
    Across this garden-chamber . . well!
But what have nightingales to do
    In gloomy England, called the free . .
(Yes, free to die in! . .) when we two
    Are sundered, singing still to me?
And still they sing, the nightingales.

V

I think I hear him, how he cried
    'My own soul's life' between their notes.
Each man has but one soul supplied,
    And that's immortal. Though his throat's
On fire with passion now, to *her*
    He can't say what to me he said!
And yet he moves her, they aver.
    The nightingales sing through my head,
The nightingales, the nightingales.

VI

He says to *her* what moves her most.
    He would not name his soul within
Her hearing,—rather pays her cost
    With praises to her lips and chin.
Man has but one soul, 'tis ordained,
    And each soul but one love, I add;
Yet souls are damned and love's profaned.
    These nightingales will sing me mad!
The nightingales, the nightingales.

VII

I marvel how the birds can sing.
  There's little difference, in their view,
Betwixt our Tuscan trees that spring
  As vital flames into the blue,
And dull round blots of foliage meant
  Like saturated sponges here
To suck the fogs up. As content
  Is *he* too in this land, 'tis clear.
And still they sing, the nightingales.

VIII

My native Florence! dear, foregone!
  I see across the Alpine ridge
How the last feast-day of St. John
  Shot rockets from Carraia bridge.
The luminous city, tall with fire,
  Trod deep down in that river of ours,
While many a boat with lamp and choir
  Skimmed birdlike over glittering towers.
I will not hear these nightingales.

IX

I seem to float, *we* seem to float
  Down Arno's stream in festive guise;
A boat strikes flame into our boat
  And up that lady seems to rise
As then she rose. The shock had flashed
  A vision on us! What a head,
What leaping eyeballs!—beauty dashed
  To splendour by a sudden dread.
And still they sing, the nightingales.

X

Too bold to sin, too weak to die;
　　Such women are so. As for me,
I would we had drowned there, he and I,
　　That moment, loving perfectly.
He had not caught her with her loosed
　　Gold ringlets . . rarer in the south . .
Nor heard the 'Grazie tanto' bruised
　　To sweetness by her English mouth.
And still they sing, the nightingales.

XI

She had not reached him at my heart
　　With her fine tongue, as snakes indeed
Kill flies; nor had I, for my part,
　　Yearned after, in my desperate need,
And followed him as he did her
　　To coasts left bitter by the tide,
Whose very nightingales, elsewhere
　　Delighting, torture and deride!
For still they sing, the nightingales.

XII

A worthless woman! mere cold clay
　　As all false things are! but so fair,
She takes the breath of men away
　　Who gaze upon her unaware.
I would not play her larcenous tricks
　　To have her looks! She lied and stole,
And spat into my lover's pure pyx
　　The rank saliva of her soul.
And still they sing, the nightingales.

XIII

I would not for her white and pink,
   Though such he likes—her grace of limb,
Though such he has praised—nor yet, I think,
   For life itself, though spent with him,
Commit such sacrilege, affront
   God's nature which is love, intrude
'Twixt two affianced souls, and hunt
   Like spiders, in the altar's wood.
I cannot bear these nightingales.

XIV

If she chose sin, some gentler guise
   She might have sinned in, so it seems:
She might have pricked out both my eyes,
   And I still seen him in my dreams!
—Or drugged me in my soup or wine,
   Nor left me angry afterward:
To die here with his hand in mine
   His breath upon me, were not hard.
(Our Lady hush these nightingales!)

XV

But set a springe for *him*, 'mio ben,'
   My only good, my first last love!—
Though Christ knows well what sin is, when
   He sees some things done they must move
Himself to wonder. Let her pass.
   I think of her by night and day.
Must *I* too join her . . out, alas! . .
   With Giulio, in each word I say?
And evermore the nightingales!

Giulio, my Giulio!—sing they so,
 And you be silent? Do I speak,
And you not hear? An arm you throw
 Round some one, and I feel so weak?
—Oh, owl-like birds! They sing for spite,
 They sing for hate, they sing for doom!
They'll sing through death who sing through night,
 They'll sing and stun me in the tomb—
The nightingales, the nightingales!

VOID IN LAW

I

Sleep, little babe, on my knee,
 Sleep, for the midnight is chill,
And the moon has died out in the tree,
 And the great human world goeth ill.
Sleep, for the wicked agree:
 Sleep, let them do as they will.
Sleep.

II

Sleep, thou hast drawn from my breast
 The last drop of milk that was good;
And now, in a dream, suck the rest,
 Lest the real should trouble thy blood.
Suck, little lips dispossessed,
 As we kiss in the air whom we would.
Sleep.

III

O lips of thy father! the same,
  So like! Very deeply they swore
When he gave me his ring and his name,
  To take back, I imagined, no more!
And now is all changed like a game,
  Though the old cards are used as of yore?
Sleep.

IV

'Void in law,' said the courts. Something wrong
  In the forms? Yet, 'Till death part us two,
I, James, take thee, Jessie,' was strong,
  And ONE witness competent. True
Such a marriage was worth an old song,
  Heard in Heaven, though, as plain as the New.
Sleep.

V

Sleep, little child, his and mine!
  Her throat has the antelope curve,
And her cheek just the colour and line
  Which fade not before him nor swerve:
Yet *she* has no child!—the divine
  Seal of right upon loves that deserve.
Sleep.

VI

My child! though the world take her part,
  Saying, 'She was the woman to choose,
He had eyes, was a man in his heart,'—
  We twain the decision refuse:
We . . . weak as I am, as thou art, . . .
  Cling on to him, never to loose.
Sleep.

VII

He thinks that, when done with this place,
  All's ended? he'll new-stamp the ore?
Yes, Cæsar's—but not in our case.
  Let him learn we are waiting before
The grave's mouth, the Heaven's gate, God's face,
  With implacable love evermore.
Sleep.

VIII

He's ours, though he kissed her but now;
  He's ours, though she kissed in reply
He's ours, though himself disavow,
  And God's universe favour the lie;
Ours to claim, ours to clasp, ours below,
  Ours above, . . . if we live, if we die.
Sleep.

IX

Ah baby, my baby, too rough
  Is my lullaby? What have I said?
Sleep? When I've wept long enough
  I shall learn to weep softly instead,
And piece with some alien stuff
  My heart to lie smooth for thy head.
Sleep.

X

Two souls met upon thee, my sweet;
  Two loves led thee out to the sun:
Alas, pretty hands, pretty feet,
  If the one who remains (only one)
Set her grief at thee, turned in a heat
  To thine enemy,—were it well done?
Sleep.

May He of the manger stand near
   And love thee! An infant He came
To His own who rejected Him here,
   But the Magi brought gifts all the same.
I hurry the cross on my Dear!
   My gifts are the griefs I declaim!
Sleep.

FIRST NEWS FROM VILLAFRANCA

I

Peace, peace, peace, do you say?
   What!—with the enemy's guns in our ears?
   With the country's wrong not rendered back?
What!—while Austria stands at bay
   In Mantua, and our Venice bears
   The cursed flag of the yellow and black?

II

Peace, peace, peace, do you say?
   And this the Mincio? Where's the fleet,
   And where's the sea? Are we all blind
Or mad with the blood shed yesterday,
   Ignoring Italy under our feet,
   And seeing things before, behind?

III

Peace, peace, peace, do you say?
   What!—uncontested, undenied?
   Because we triumph, we succumb?
A pair of Emperors stand in the way,
   (One of whom is a man, beside)
To sign and seal our cannons dumb?

IV

No, not Napoleon!—he who mused
  At Paris, and at Milan spake,
  And at Solferino led the fight:
Not he we trusted, honoured, used
  Our hope and hearts for . . till they break—
  Even so, you tell us . . in his sight.

V

Peace, peace, is still your word?
  We say you lie then!—that is plain.
  There *is* no peace, and shall be none.
Our very dead would cry 'Absurd!'
  And clamour that they died in vain,
  And whine to come back to the sun.

VI

Hush! more reverence for the dead!
  They've done the most for Italy
  Evermore since the earth was fair.
Now would that *we* had died instead,
  Still dreaming peace meant liberty,
  And did not, could not mean despair.

VII

Peace, you say?—yes, peace, in truth!
  But such a peace as the ear can achieve
  'Twixt the rifle's click and the rush of the ball,
'Twixt the tiger's spring and the crunch of the tooth,
  'Twixt the dying atheist's negative
  And God's face—waiting, after all!

THE FORCED RECRUIT

SOLFERINO 1859

I

In the ranks of the Austrian you found him,
   He died with his face to you all;
Yet bury him here where around him
   You honour your bravest that fall.

II

Venetian, fair-featured and slender,
   He lies shot to death in his youth,
With a smile on his lips over-tender
   For any mere soldier's dead mouth.

III

No stranger, and yet not a traitor,
   Though alien the cloth on his breast,
Underneath it how seldom a greater
   Young heart, has a shot sent to rest!

IV

By your enemy tortured and goaded
   To march with them, stand in their file,
His musket (see) never was loaded,
   He facing your guns with that smile!

V

As orphans yearn on to their mothers,
   He yearned to your patriot bands;—
'Let me die for our Italy, brothers,
   If not in your ranks, by your hands!

'Aim straightly, fire steadily! spare me
    A ball in the body which may
Deliver my heart here, and tear me
    This badge of the Austrian away!'

So thought he, so died he this morning.
    What then? many others have died.
Aye, but easy for men to die scorning
    The death-stroke, who fought side by side—

One tricolor floating above them;
    Struck down 'mid triumphant acclaims
Of an Italy rescued to love them
    And blazon the brass with their names.

But he,—without witness or honour,
    Mixed, shamed in his country's regard,
With the tyrants who march in upon her,
    Died faithful and passive: 'twas hard.

'Twas sublime. In a cruel restriction
    Cut off from the guerdon of sons,
With most filial obedience, conviction,
    His soul kissed the lips of her guns.

That moves you? Nay, grudge not to show it,
   While digging a grave for him here:
The others who died, says your poet,
   Have glory,—let *him* have a tear.

MOTHER AND POET

(TURIN, AFTER NEWS FROM GAETA, 1861)

I

Dead! One of them shot by the sea in the east,
   And one of them shot in the west by the sea.
Dead! both my boys! When you sit at the feast
   And are wanting a great song for Italy free,
      Let none look at *me!*

II

Yet I was a poetess only last year,
   And good at my art, for a woman, men said;
But *this* woman, *this*, who is agonised here,
   —The east sea and west sea rhyme on in her head
      For ever instead.

III

What art can a woman be good at? Oh, vain!
   What art *is* she good at, but hurting her breast
With the milk-teeth of babes, and a smile at the pain?
   Ah boys, how you hurt! you were strong as you pressed,
      And I proud, by that test.

IV

What art's for a woman? To hold on her knees
    Both darlings! to feel all their arms round her throat,
Cling, strangle a little! to sew by degrees
    And 'broider the long-clothes and neat little coat;
        To dream and to doat.

V

To teach them . . . It stings there! *I* made them indeed
    Speak plain the word *country*. *I* taught them, no doubt,
That a country's a thing men should die for at need.
    I prated of liberty, rights, and about
        The tyrant cast out.

VI

And when their eyes flashed . . . O my beautiful eyes! . . .
    I exulted; nay, let them go forth at the wheels
Of the guns, and denied not. But then the surprise
    When one sits quite alone! Then one weeps, then one kneels!
        God, how the house feels!

VII

At first, happy news came, in gay letters moiled
    With my kisses,—of camp-life and glory, and how
They both loved me; and, soon coming home to be spoiled
    In return would fan off every fly from my brow
        With their green laurel-bough.

VIII

Then was triumph at Turin: 'Ancona was free!'
    And some one came out of the cheers in the street,
With a face pale as stone, to say something to me.
    My Guido was dead! I fell down at his feet,
        While they cheered in the street.

IX

I bore it; friends soothed me; my grief looked sublime
    As the ransom of Italy. One boy remained
To be leant on and walked with, recalling the time
    When the first grew immortal, while both of us strained
        To the height he had gained.

X

And letters still came, shorter, sadder, more strong,
    Writ now but in one hand, 'I was not to faint,—
One loved me for two—would be with me ere long:
    And *Viva l' Italia!—he* died for, our saint,
        Who forbids our complaint.'

XI

My Nanni would add, 'he was safe, and aware
    Of a presence that turned off the balls,—was imprest
It was Guido himself, who knew what I could bear,
    And how 'twas impossible, quite dispossessed
        To live on for the rest.'

XII

On which, without pause, up the telegraph line
    Swept smoothly the next news from Gaeta:—*Shot.*
Tell his mother. Ah, ah, 'his,' 'their' mother,—not 'mine,'
    No voice says '*My* mother' again to me. What!
        You think Guido forgot?

XIII

Are souls straight so happy that, dizzy with Heaven,
    They drop earth's affections, conceive not of woe?
I think not. Themselves were too lately forgiven
    Through THAT Love and Sorrow which reconciled so
        The Above and Below.

XIV

O Christ of the five wounds, who look'dst through the dark
     To the face of Thy mother! consider, I pray,
How we common mothers stand desolate, mark,
     Whose sons, not being Christs, die with eyes turned away,
          And no last word to say!

XV

Both boys dead? but that's out of nature. We all
     Have been patriots, yet each house must always keep one.
'Twere imbecile, hewing out roads to a wall;
     And, when Italy's made, for what end is it done
          If we have not a son?

XVI

Ah, ah, ah! when Gaeta's taken, what then?
     When the fair wicked queen sits no more at her sport
Of the fire-balls of death crashing souls out of men?
     When the guns of Cavalli with final retort
          Have cut the game short?

XVII

When Venice and Rome keep their new jubilee,
     When your flag takes all heaven for its white, green, and red,
When *you* have your country from mountain to sea,
     When King Victor has Italy's crown on his head,
          (And *I* have my Dead)—

XVIII

What then? Do not mock me. Ah, ring your bells low,
     And burn your lights faintly! *My* country is *there*,
Above the star pricked by the last peak of snow:
     My Italy's THERE, with my brave civic Pair,
          To disfranchise despair!

XIX

Forgive me. Some women bear children in strength,
    And bite back the cry of their pain in self-scorn;
But the birth-pangs of nations will wring us at length
    Into wail such as this—and we sit on forlorn
        When the man-child is born.

XX

Dead! One of them shot by the sea in the east,
    And one of them shot in the west by the sea.
Both! both my boys! If in keeping the feast
    You want a great song for your Italy free,
        Let none look at *me!*

A MUSICAL INSTRUMENT

I

What was he doing, the great god Pan,
    Down in the reeds by the river?
Spreading ruin and scattering ban,
Splashing and paddling with hoofs of a goat,
And breaking the golden lilies afloat
    With the dragon-fly on the river.

II

He tore out a reed, the great god Pan,
    From the deep cool bed of the river:
The limpid water turbidly ran,
And the broken lilies a-dying lay,
And the dragon-fly had fled away,
    Ere he brought it out of the river.

III

High on the shore sate the great god Pan,
　　While turbidly flowed the river;
And hacked and hewed as a great god can,
With his hard bleak steel at the patient reed,
Till there was not a sign of a leaf indeed
　　To prove it fresh from the river.

IV

He cut it short, did the great god Pan,
　　(How tall it stood in the river!)
Then drew the pith, like the heart of a man,
Steadily from the outside ring,
And notched the poor dry empty thing
　　In holes, as he sate by the river.

V

'This is the way,' laughed the great god Pan,
　　(Laughed while he sate by the river,)
'The only way, since gods began
To make sweet music, they could succeed.'
Then, dropping his mouth to a hole in the reed,
　　He blew in power by the river.

VI

Sweet, sweet, sweet, O Pan!
　　Piercing sweet by the river!
Blinding sweet, O great god Pan!
The sun on the hill forgot to die,
And the lilies revived, and the dragon-fly
　　Came back to dream on the river.

Yet half a beast is the great god Pan,
　　To laugh as he sits by the river,
Making a poet out of a man:
The true gods sigh for the cost and pain,—
For the reed which grows nevermore again
　　As a reed with the reeds in the river.

THE NORTH AND THE SOUTH

ROME, MAY 1861

I

'Now give us lands where the olives grow,'
　　Cried the North to the South,
'Where the sun with a golden mouth can blow
Blue bubbles of grapes down a vineyard-row!'
　　Cried the North to the South.

II

'Now give us men from the sunless plain,'
　　Cried the South to the North,
'By need of work in the snow and the rain,
Made strong, and brave by familiar pain!'
　　Cried the South to the North.

III

'Give lucider hills and intenser seas,'
　　Said the North to the South,
'Since ever by symbols and bright degrees
'Art, childlike, climbs to the dear Lord's knees,'
　　Said the North to the South.

IV

'Give strenuous souls for belief and prayer,'
    Said the South to the North,
'That stand in the dark on the lowest stair,
While affirming of God, "He is certainly there,"'
    Said the South to the North.

V

'Yet oh, for the skies that are softer and higher!'
    Sighed the North to the South;
'For the flowers that blaze, and the trees that aspire,
And the insects made of a song or a fire!'
    Sighed the North to the South.

VI

'And oh, for a seer to discern the same!'
    Sighed the South to the North!
'For a poet's tongue of baptismal flame,
To call the tree or the flower by its name!'
    Sighed the South to the North.

VII

The North sent therefore a man of men,
    As a grace to the South;
And thus to Rome came Andersen.
—'*Alas, but must you take him again?*'
    Said the South to the North.

Index of Poems